THE CRITICAL DIFFERENCE

Barbara Johnson teaches in the departments of French and Comparative Literature at Yale University. She is the author of *Défigurations: du langage poétique* and translator of Jacques Derrida's *La Dissémination*.

THE CRITICAL DIFFERENCE

ESSAYS IN THE CONTEMPORARY
RHETORIC OF READING

BARBARA JOHNSON

THE JOHNS HOPKINS UNIVERSITY PRESS
BALTIMORE AND LONDON

This book has been brought to publication with the generous assistance of the
Andrew W. Mellon Foundation.

Originally published, 1980
Second printing, 1982

Johns Hopkins Paperbacks edition, 1985

The Johns Hopkins University Press
701 West 40th Street
Baltimore, Maryland 21211
The Johns Hopkins Press Ltd., London

Library of Congress Cataloging in Publication Data
Johnson, Barbara, 1947–
    The critical difference.

    Includes bibliographical references and index.
    1. Criticism. 2. Reading. 3. Literature.
I. Title.
PN81.J56   1981   801'.95   80-21533
ISBN 0-8018-2458-3 (hardcover)
ISBN 0-8018-2728-0 (paperback)

   "Melville's Fist: The Execution of *Billy Budd*," reprinted from *Studies in Romanticism* vol. 18, no. 4, 1979, by permission of the Trustees of Boston University.
   "Poetry and Its Double," translated and modified by the author, reprinted, by permission, from *Défigurations: du langage poétique* by Barbara Johnson. Copyright Flammarion, 1979.
   "Poetry and Performative Language," reprinted, by permission, from *Yale French Studies* no. 54, 1977.
   "The Frame of Reference: Poe, Lacan, Derrida," reprinted, by permission, from *Yale French Studies,* no. 55/56, 1978.

Asked by his wife whether he wants to have his bowling shoes laced over or laced under, Archie Bunker answers with a question: "What's the difference?" Being a reader of sublime simplicity, his wife replies by patiently explaining the difference between lacing over and lacing under, whatever this may be, but provokes only ire. "What's the difference?" did not ask for difference but means instead "I don't give a damn what the difference is." The same grammatical pattern engenders two meanings that are mutually exclusive: the literal meaning asks for the concept (difference) whose existence is denied by the figurative meaning. As long as we are talking about bowling shoes, the consequences are relatively trivial; Archie Bunker, who is a great believer in the authority of origins (as long, of course, as they are the right origins) muddles along in a world where literal and figurative meanings get in each other's way, though not without discomforts. But suppose that it is a *de*-bunker rather than a "Bunker", and a de-bunker of the arche (or origin), an archie Debunker such as Nietzsche or Jacques Derrida, for instance, who asks the question "What is the Difference"—and we cannot even tell from his grammar whether he "really" wants to know "what" difference is or is just telling us that we shouldn't even try to find out. Confronted with the question of the difference between grammar and rhetoric, grammar allows us to ask the question, but the sentence by means of which we ask it may deny the very possibility of asking. For what is the use of asking, I ask, when we cannot even authoritatively decide whether a question asks or doesn't ask?

—Paul de Man, *Allegories of Reading*

Contents

Opening Remarks

Difference. 1. The condition or degree of being unlike, dissimilar, or diverse; disparity, variation. 2. A specific point of disparity or unlikeness; an instance of variation. 3. *Archaic.* A distinct mark or peculiarity. 4. A disagreement; controversy; quarrel. 5. Discrimination; distinction. 6. Mathematics: a) the amount by which one quantity is greater or less than another. b) The amount that remains after one quantity is subtracted from another. Also called "remainder." (From Latin *differre*, to carry in different directions: *dis*, apart + *ferre*, to carry).

Critical. 1. Inclined to judge severely; given to censuring. 2. Characterized by careful and exact evaluation and judgment. 3. Of, pertaining to, or characteristic of critics or criticism. 4. Forming, or of the nature of, a crisis; crucial. 5. Fraught with danger or risk; perilous. (From Latin *criticus*, "decisive," from Greek *kritikos*, able to discern, critical, from *kritos*, separated, chosen, from *krinein*, to separate, choose.)

—American Heritage Dictionary

What, indeed, *is* the "difference" here?

This question can perhaps be approached by way of the relation between the two definitions I have quoted above. On the one hand, the two seemingly different words *critical* and *difference* are surprisingly alike; they both range from an objective, disinterested function of discrimination ("distinction," "careful and exact evaluation") to an argumentative or agonistic function of condemnation ("a disagreement or quarrel," "judging severely, censuring"). Both can have the urgency of a crisis or the tranquillity of a taxonomy, and both derive from words meaning the same thing: "to carry apart," "to separate." The difference between *difference* and *critical*, in other words, is not as clear and distinct as we might have been tempted to think.

On the other hand, within each definition, the historical process of drifting away from the Greek or Latin root has opened up within each word a range of meanings that render it different from itself. Each of the two words can name either a dynamic, conflictual opposition or a static, descriptive distinction. And each can refer both to the fact of division and to the nature of the differends.

The problem of difference can thus be seen both as an uncertainty over separability and as a drifting apart within identity. And the very fact that it is impossible to know whether something constitutes description or disagreement, information or censure, is perhaps ultimately the most problematic and critical difference of all. For it is precisely in the nature of difference that it consist in the engendering of uncertainty not only over its nature but also over the danger or usefulness of its very propagation. What is often most fundamentally disagreed upon is whether a disagreement arises out of the complexities of fact or out of the impulses of power.

The essays collected in this volume have as their common focus the problem of this type of "difference" as it structures and undermines the act of reading. But it should already be clear that the meaning of the words *difference* and *reading* cannot be taken for granted. In each essay, they function as two unknowns in a textual equation whose unresolvability is matched only by its ability to engender more textuality.

In each essay, the text or its pattern of previous readings is seen to be setting up a network of differences into which the reader is lured with a promise of comprehension. The oppositions dealt with here, among others, are: masculine/feminine, literature/criticism (Chapter 1); sexuality/textuality (Chapter 2); prose/poetry, original/repetition (Chapter 3); poetry/theory, performative/constative, reference/self-reference (Chapter 4); clarity/obscurity, science/literature, syntax/semantics (Chapter 5); naive/ironic, murder/error, criminal/victim/judge (Chapter 6); and, finally, literature/psychoanalysis/philosophy, and all the binary and ternary oppositions this entails, including a discussion of the applicability of such numerical formulations to the ways in which difference intervenes in interpretation (Chapter 7).

Reading, here, proceeds by identifying and dismantling differences by means of other differences that cannot be fully identified or dismantled. The starting point is often a binary difference that is subsequently shown to be an illusion created by the workings of differences much harder to pin down. The differences *between* entities (prose and poetry, man and woman, literature and theory, guilt and innocence) are shown to be based on a repression of differences *within* entities, ways in which an entity differs from itself. But the way in which a text thus differs from itself is never simple: it has a certain rigorous, contradictory logic whose effects can, up to a certain point, be read. The "deconstruction" of a binary opposition is thus not an annihilation of all values or differences; it is an attempt to follow the subtle, powerful effects of differences already at work within the illusion of a binary opposition. It is Baudelaire's prose poem, for example, that, in standing in binary opposition to the verse poem it rewrites, makes visible the way in which that verse poem already differed from what it had seemed to be. If, however, binary oppositions in this book thus play the role of the critical fall guy, it is not because one must try at all costs to go beyond them. The very impulse to "go beyond" is an impulse structured by a binary opposition between oneself and what one attempts to leave behind. Far from eliminating binary oppositions from the critical vocabulary, one can only show that binary difference does not function as one thinks it does and that certain subversions that seem to befall it in the critical narrative are logically prior to it and necessary in its very construction. Difference is a form of *work* to the extent that it *plays* beyond the control of any subject: it is, in fact, that without which no subject could ever be constituted.

In his essay entitled "La différance," Jacques Derrida emphasizes the inseparability of the spatial and temporal dynamics of difference. In coining the word *différance* with an *a,* he combines the two senses of the French verb *différer*—to differ and to defer (postpone)—into one designation for what both subverts and produces the illusion of presence, identity, and consciousness:

> Differance is what ensures that the movement of signification be possible only if each so-called "present" element, each element that appears on the stage of presence, is related to something other than itself. . . . Some interval or gap must separate it from what is not itself in order for it to be itself, but that interval which constitutes it in the present must also by the same token divide the present in itself, thus cutting through . . . everything that can be thought out on the basis of the present . . . , singularly the "substance" or the "subject."[1]

As this quotation from Derrida makes clear, the present volume is also the record of one reader's struggles to come to grips with the problems posed by contemporary so-called deconstructive critical theory. Difference is, of course, at work within the very discourse of theory itself. Indeed, it is precisely contemporary theory that has made us so aware of this. Theoretical pronouncements therefore do not stand here as instruments to be used in mastering literary structures. On the contrary, it is through contact with literature that theoretical tools are useful precisely to the extent that they thereby change and dissolve in the hands of the user. Theory is here often the straight man whose precarious rectitude and hidden risibility, passion, and pathos are precisely what literature has somehow already foreseen. For literature stages the modes of its own misreading, making visible the literarity of the heart of theory and rendering the effects of its project of understanding unpredictable. The rhetorical subversion of theory by its own discourse does not, however, prevent it from generating effects; indeed, it is precisely the way theory misses its target that produces incalculable and interesting effects elsewhere.[2]

If this volume has any overall preoccupation, it is perhaps the importance of the functioning of *what is not known* in literature or theory. Far from being a negative or nonexistent factor, what is not known is often the unseen motivating force behind the very deployment of meaning. The power of ignorance, blindness, uncertainty, or misreading is often all the more redoubtable for not being perceived as such. Literature, it seems to me, is the discourse most preoccupied with the unknown, but not in the sense in which such a statement is usually understood. The "unknown" is not what lies beyond the limits of knowledge, some unreachable, sacred, ineffable point toward which we vainly yearn. It lies, rather, in the oversights and slip-ups that structure our lives in the same way that an X makes it possible to articulate an algebraic equation. What literature often seems to tell us is the consequences of the way in which what is not known is not seen as unknown. It is not, in the final analysis, what you don't know that can or cannot hurt you. It is what you don't *know* you don't know that spins out and entangles "that perpetual error we call life."

PART ONE:
SEXUALITY
AND DIFFERENCE

1. The Critical Difference: BartheS/BalZac

Literary criticism as such can perhaps be called the art of rereading. I would therefore like to begin by quoting the remarks about rereading made by Roland Barthes in *S/Z:*

> Rereading, an operation contrary to the commercial and ideological habits of our society, which would have us "throw away" the story once it has been consumed ("devoured"), so that we can then move on to another story, buy another book, and which is tolerated only in certain marginal categories of readers (children, old people, and professors), rereading is here suggested at the outset, for it alone saves the text from repetition (*those who fail to reread are obliged to read the same story everywhere*).[1] (Emphasis mine)

What does this paradoxical statement imply? First, it implies that a single reading is composed of the already-read, that what we can see in a text the first time is already in us, not in it; in us insofar as we ourselves are a stereotype, an already-read text; and in the text only to the extent that the already-read is that aspect of a text that it must have in common with its reader in order for it to be readable at all. When we read a text once, in other words, we can see in it only what we have already learned to see before.

Secondly, the statement that those who do not reread must read the same story everywhere involves a reversal of the usual properties of the words *same* and *different*. Here, it is the consuming of different stories that is equated with the repetition of the same, while it is the rereading of the same that engenders what Barthes calls the "text's difference." This critical concept of difference, which has been valorized both by Saussurian linguistics and by the Nietzschean tradition in philosophy—particularly the work of Jacques Derrida—is crucial to the practice of what is called deconstructive criticism. I would therefore like to examine here some of its implications and functions.

3

In a sense, it could be said that to make a critical difference is the object of all criticism as such. The very word *criticism* comes from the Greek verb *krinein*, "to separate or choose," that is, to differentiate. The critic not only seeks to establish standards for evaluating the differences between texts but also tries to perceive something uniquely different within each text he reads and in so doing to establish his own individual difference from other critics. But this is not quite what Barthes means when he speaks of the text's difference. On the first page of *S/Z*, he writes:

> This difference is not, obviously, some complete, irreducible quality (according to a mythic view of literary creation), it is not what designates the individuality of each text, what names, signs, finishes off each work with a flourish; on the contrary, it is a difference which does not stop and which is articulated upon the infinity of texts, of languages, of systems: a difference of which each text is the return. (P. 3)

In other words, a text's difference is not its uniqueness, its special identity. It is the text's way of differing from itself. And this difference is perceived only in the act of rereading. It is the way in which the text's signifying energy becomes unbound, to use Freud's term, through the process of repetition, which is the return not of sameness but of difference. Difference, in other words, is not what distinguishes one identity from another. It is not a difference between (or at least not between independent units), but a difference within. Far from constituting the text's unique identity, it is that which subverts the very idea of identity, infinitely deferring the possibility of adding up the sum of a text's parts or meanings and reaching a totalized, integrated whole.

Let me illustrate this idea further by turning for a moment to Rousseau's *Confessions*. Rousseau's opening statement about himself is precisely an affirmation of difference: "I am unlike anyone I have ever met; I will even venture to say that I am like no one in the whole world. I may be no better, but at least I am different" (Penguin edition, 1954, p. 17). Now, this can be read as an unequivocal assertion of uniqueness, of difference between Rousseau and the whole rest of the world. This is the boast on which the book is based. But in what does the uniqueness of this self consist? It is not long before we find out: "There are times when I am so unlike myself that I might be taken for someone else of an entirely opposite character" (p. 126). "In me are united two almost irreconcilable characteristics, though in what way I cannot imagine" (p. 112). In other words, this story of the self's difference from others inevitably becomes the story of its own unbridgeable difference from itself. Difference is not engendered in the space between identities; it is what makes all totalization of the identity of a self or the meaning of a text impossible.

It is this type of textual difference that informs the process of deconstructive criticism. *Deconstruction* is not synonymous with *destruction,* however. It is in fact much closer to the original meaning of the word *analysis,* which etymologically means "to undo"—a virtual synonym for "to de-construct." The de-construction of a text does not proceed by random doubt or arbitrary subversion, but by the careful teasing out of warring forces of signification within the text itself. If anything is destroyed in a deconstructive reading, it is not the text, but the claim to unequivocal domination of one mode of signifying over another. A deconstructive reading is a reading that analyzes the specificity of a text's critical difference from itself.

I have chosen to approach this question of critical difference by way of Barthes's *S/Z* for three reasons:

1. Barthes sets up a critical value system explicitly based on the paradigm of difference, and in the process works out one of the earliest, most influential, and most lucid and forceful syntheses of contemporary French theoretical thought;

2. The Balzac story that Barthes chooses to analyze in *S/Z* is itself in a way a study of difference—a subversive and unsettling formulation of the question of sexual difference;

3. The confrontation between Barthes and Balzac may have something to say about the critical differences between theory and practice, on the one hand, and between literature and criticism, on the other.

I shall begin by recalling the manner in which Barthes outlines his value system:

> Our evaluation can be linked only to a practice, and this practice is that of writing. On the one hand, there is what it is possible to write, and on the other, what it is no longer possible to write. . . . What evaluation finds is precisely this value: what can be written (rewritten) today: the *writerly* [*le scriptible*]. Why is the writerly our value? Because the goal of literary work (of literature as work) is to make the reader no longer a consumer, but a producer of the text. . . . Opposite the writerly text is its countervalue, its negative, reactive value: what can be read, but not written: the *readerly* [*le lisible*]. We call any readerly text a classic text. (P. 4)

Here, then, is the major polarity that Barthes sets up as a tool for evaluating texts: the readerly versus the writerly. The readerly is defined as a product consumed by the reader; the writerly is a process of production in which the reader becomes a producer: it is "ourselves writing." The readerly is constrained by considerations of representation:

it is irreversible, "natural," decidable, continuous, totalizable, and unified into a coherent whole based on the signified. The writerly is infinitely plural and open to the free play of signifiers and of difference, unconstrained by representative considerations, and transgressive of any desire for decidable, unified, totalized meaning.

With this value system, one would naturally expect to find Barthes going on to extoll the play of infinite plurality in some Joycean or Mallarméan piece of writerly obscurity, but no; he turns to Balzac, one of the most readerly of readerly writers, as Barthes himself insists. Why then does Barthes choose to talk about Balzac? Barthes skillfully avoids confronting this question. But perhaps it is precisely the way in which Barthes' choice of Balzac does not follow logically from his value system—that is, the way in which Barthes somehow differs from himself—which opens up the critical difference we must analyze here.

Although Balzac's text apparently represents for Barthes the negative, readerly end of the hierarchy, Barthes's treatment of it does seem to illustrate all the characteristics of the positive, writerly end. In the first place, one cannot help but be struck by the plurality of Barthes's text, with its numerous sizes of print, its "systematic use of digression," and its successive superposable versions of the same but different story, from the initial reproduction of Girodet's *Endymion* to the four appendixes, which repeat the book's contents in different forms. The reading technique proper also obeys the demand for fragmentation and pluralization, and consists of "manhandling" the text:

> What we seek is to sketch the stereographic space of writing (which will here be a classic, readerly writing). The commentary, based on the affirmation of the plural, cannot work with "respect" to the text; the tutor text will ceaselessly be broken, interrupted without any regard for its natural divisions . . . the work of the commentary, once it is separated from any ideology of totality, consists precisely in *manhandling* the text, *interrupting* it [lui couper la parole]. What is thereby denied is not the *quality* of the text (here incomparable) but its "naturalness." (P. 15)

Barthes goes on to divide the story diachronically into 561 fragments called *lexias* and synchronically into five so-called voices or codes, thus transforming the text into a "complex network" with "multiple entrances and exits."

The purposes of these cuts and codes is to pluralize the reader's intake, to effect a resistance to the reader's desire to restructure the text into large, ordered masses of meaning: "If we want to remain attentive to the plural of a text . . . we must renounce structuring this text in large masses, as was done by classical rhetoric and by secondary-school explication: no construction of the text" (pp. 11–12). In leaving the text as heterogeneous and discontinuous as possible, in attempting to avoid the repressiveness of the attempt to dominate the message and force the text into a single ultimate meaning, Barthes thus works a maximum of disintegrative violence and a minimum of integrative violence. The question to ask is whether this "anti-constructionist" (as opposed to "de-constructionist") fidelity to the fragmented signifier succeeds in laying bare the functional plurality of Balzac's text, or whether in the final analysis a certain systematic level of textual difference is not also lost and flattened by Barthes's refusal to reorder or reconstruct the text.

Let us now turn to Balzac's *Sarrasine* itself. The story is divided into two parts: the story of the telling and the telling of the story. In the first part, the narrator attempts to seduce a beautiful Marquise by telling her the second part; that is, he wants to exchange narrative knowledge for carnal knowledge. The lady wants to know the secret of the mysterious old man at the party, and the narrator wants to know the lady. Story-telling, as Barthes points out, is thus not an innocent, neutral activity, but rather part of a bargain, an act of seduction. But here the bargain is not kept; the deal backfires. The knowledge the lady has acquired, far from bringing about her surrender, prevents it. In fact, the last thing she says is: "No one will have *known* me."

It is obvious that the key to this failure of the bargain lies in the content of the story used to fulfill it. That story is about the passion of the sculptor Sarrasine for the opera singer La Zambinella, and is based not on knowledge but on ignorance: the sculptor's ignorance of the Italian custom of using castrated men instead of women to play the soprano parts on the operatic stage. The sculptor, who had seen in La Zambinella the perfect female body for the first time realized in one person, a veritable Pygmalion's statue come to life, finds out that this image of feminine perfection literally has been carved by a knife, not in stone but in the flesh itself. He who had proclaimed his willingness to die for his love ends up doing just that, killed by La Zambinella's protector.

How is it that the telling of this sordid little tale ends up subverting the very bargain it was intended to fulfill? Barthes's answer to this is clear: "castration is contagious"—"contaminated by the castration she has just been told about, [the Marquise] impels the narrator into it" (p. 36).

What is interesting about this story of seduction and castration is the way in which it unexpectedly reflects upon Barthes's own critical value system. For in announcing that "the tutor text will ceaselessly be broken, interrupted without any regard for its natural divisions," is

Barthes not implicitly privileging something like castration over what he calls the "ideology of totality"? "If the text is subject to some form," he writes, "this form is not unitary . . . , finite; it is the fragment, the slice, the cut up or erased network" (p. 20; translation modified). Indeed, might it not be possible to read Balzac's opposition between the ideal woman and the castrato as metaphorically assimilable to Barthes's opposition between the readerly and the writerly? Like the readerly text, Sarrasine's deluded image of La Zambinella is a glorification of perfect unity and wholeness:

> At that instant he marveled at the ideal beauty he had hitherto sought in life, seeking in one often unworthy model the roundness of a perfect leg; in another, the curve of a breast; in another, white shoulders; finally taking some girl's neck, some woman's hands, and some child's smooth knees, without ever having encountered under the cold Parisian sky the rich, sweet creations of ancient Greece. La Zambinella displayed to him, *united*, living, and delicate, those exquisite female forms he so ardently desired. (Pp. 237–38; emphasis mine)

But like the writerly text, Zambinella is actually fragmented, unnatural, and sexually undecidable. Like the readerly, the soprano is a product to be "devoured" ("With his eyes, Sarrasine devoured Pygmalion's statue, come down from its pedestal" [p. 238]), while, like the writerly, castration is a process of production, an active and violent indetermination. The soprano's appearance seems to embody the very essence of "woman" as a *signified* ("This was woman herself . . ." [p. 248]), while the castrato's reality, like the writerly text, is a mere play of signifiers, emptied of any ultimate signified, robbed of what the text calls a "heart": "I have no heart," says Zambinella, "the stage where you saw me . . . is my life, I have no other" (p. 247).

Here, then, is the first answer to the question of why Barthes might have chosen this text; it explicitly thematizes the opposition between unity and fragmentation, between the idealized signified and the discontinuous empty play of signifiers, which underlies his opposition between the readerly and the writerly. The traditional value system that Barthes is attempting to reverse is thus already mapped out within the text he analyzes. Three questions, however, immediately present themselves: (1) Does Balzac's story really uphold the unambiguousness of the readerly values to which Barthes relegates it? (2) Does Balzac simply regard ideal beauty as a lost paradise and castration as a horrible tragedy? (3) If Barthes is really attempting to demystify the ideology of totality, and if his critical strategy implicitly gives a positive value to castration, why does his analysis of Balzac's text still seem to take castration at face value as an unmitigated and catastrophic horror?

In order to answer these questions, let us take another look at

Balzac's story. To regard castration as the ultimate narrative revelation and as the unequivocal cause of Sarrasine's tragedy, as Barthes repeatedly does, is to read the story more or less from Sarrasine's point of view. It is in fact Barthes's very attempt to pluralize the text which thus restricts his perspective; however "disrespectfully" he may cut up or manhandle the story, his reading remains to a large extent dependent on the linearity of the signifier and thus on the successive unfoldings of the truth of castration to Sarrasine and to the reader. Sarrasine's ignorance, however, is not only a simple lack of knowledge but also a blindness to the injustice that is being done to him and that he is also potentially doing to the other. This does not mean that Balzac's story is a plea for the prevention of cruelty to castrati, but that the failure of the couple to unite can perhaps not simply be attributed to the literal fact of castration. Let us therefore examine the nature of Sarrasine's passion more closely.

Upon seeing La Zambinella for the first time, Sarrasine exclaims: "To be loved by her, or to die!" (p. 238). This alternative places all of the energy of the passion not on the object, La Zambinella, but on the subject, Sarrasine. To be loved, or to die; to exist as the desired object, or not to exist at all. What is at stake is not the union between two people, but the narcissistic awakening of one. Seeing La Zambinella is Sarrasine's first experience of *himself* as an object of love. By means of the image of sculpturesque perfection, Sarrasine thus falls in love with none other than himself. Balzac's fictional narrator makes explicit the narcissistic character of Sarrasine's passion and at the same time nostalgically identifies with it himself when he calls it "this golden age of love, during which we are happy almost by ourselves" (p. 240). Sarrasine contents himself with La Zambinella as the product of his own sculptor's imagination ("This was more than a woman, this was a masterpiece!" [p. 238]) and does not seek to find out who she is in reality ("As he began to realize that he would soon have to act . . . to ponder, in short, on ways to see her, speak to her, these great, ambitious thoughts made his heart swell so painfully that he put them off until later, deriving as much satisfaction from his physical suffering as he did from his intellectual pleasures" [p. 240]). When the sculptor is finally forced into the presence of his beloved, he reads in her only the proof of his own masculinity—she is the ideal woman, therefore he is the ideal man. When Sarrasine sees La Zambinella shudder at the pop of a cork, he is charmed by her weakness and says, "My strength [puissance] is your shield" (p. 244). La Zambinella's weakness is thus the inverted mirror image of Sarrasine's potency. In this narcissistic system, the difference between the sexes is based on symmetry, and it is precisely the castrato that Sarrasine does indeed love—the image of the lack of what he thereby thinks he himself possesses. When Sarrasine says that he would not be able to love a strong woman, he is saying in effect that he would be unable to love anyone who was not his symmetrical opposite and the proof of his masculinity. This is to say that even if La Zambinella *had* been a real woman, Sarrasine's love would be a refusal to deal with her as a real other. This type of narcissism is in fact just as contagious in the story as castration: the Marquise sees the narcissistic delusion inherent in the narrator's own passion, and, banteringly foreshadowing one of the reasons for her ultimate refusal, protests: "Oh, you fashion me to your own taste. What tyranny! You don't want me for myself!" (p. 233).

Sarrasine cannot listen to the other as other. Even when Zambinella suggests the truth by means of a series of equivocal remarks culminating in the question (directed toward Sarrasine's offers to sacrifice everything for love)—"And if I were not a woman?"—Sarrasine cries: "What a joke! Do you think you can deceive an artist's eye?" (p. 247). Sarrasine's strength is thus a shield *against* La Zambinella, not *for* her. He creates her as his own symmetrical opposite and through her loves only himself. This is why the revelation of the truth is fatal. The castrato is simultaneously outside the difference between the sexes as well as representing the literalization of its illusory symmetry. He subverts the desire for symmetrical, binary difference by fulfilling it. He destroys Sarrasine's reassuring masculinity by revealing that it is based on castration. But Sarrasine's realization that he himself is thereby castrated, that he is looking at his true mirror image, is still blind to the fact that he had never been capable of loving in the first place. His love was from the beginning the cancellation and castration of the other.

What Sarrasine dies of, then, is precisely a failure to *reread* in the exact sense with which we began this chapter. What he devours so eagerly in La Zambinella is actually located within himself: a collection of sculpturesque clichés about feminine beauty and his own narcissism. In thinking that he knows where difference is located—between the sexes—he is blind to a difference that cannot be situated between, but only within. In Balzac's story, castration thus stands as the literalization of the "difference within" which prevents any subject from coinciding with itself. In Derrida's terms, Sarrasine reads the opera singer as pure voice ("his passion for La Zambinella's voice" [p. 241]), as an illusion of imaginary immediacy ("The distance between himself and La Zambinella had ceased to exist, he possessed her" [p. 239]), as a perfectly readable, motivated sign ("Do you think you can deceive an artist's eye?"), as full and transparent Logos, whereas she is the very image of the empty and arbitrary sign, of writing inhabited by its own irreducible difference from itself. And it can be seen that the failure to reread is hardly a trivial matter: for Sarrasine, it is fatal.

Balzac's text thus itself demystifies the logocentric blindness inherent in Sarrasine's reading of the Zambinellian text. But if Sarrasine's view of La Zambinella as an image of perfect wholeness and unequivocal femininity is analogous to the classic, readerly conception of literature according to Barthes's definition, then Balzac's text has already worked out the same type of deconstruction of the readerly ideal as that which Barthes is trying to accomplish as if it stood in opposition to the classic text. In other words, Balzac's text already "knows" the limits and blindnesses of the readerly, which it personifies in Sarrasine. Balzac has already in a sense done Barthes's work for him. The readerly text is itself nothing other than a deconstruction of the readerly text.

But at the same time, Balzac's text does not operate a simple reversal of the readerly hierarchy; Balzac does not proclaim castration as the truth behind the readerly's blindness in as unequivocal a way as Barthes's own unequivocality would lead one to believe. For every time Balzac's text is about to use the word *castration,* it leaves a blank instead. "Ah, you are a woman," cries Sarrasine in despair; "for even a . . ." He breaks off. "No," he continues, "he would not be so cowardly" (p. 251). Balzac repeatedly castrates his text of the word *castration.* Far from being the unequivocal answer to the text's enigma, castration is the way in which the enigma's answer is withheld. Castration is what the story must, and cannot, say. But what Barthes does in his reading is to label these textual blanks "taboo on the word castrato" (pp. 75, 177, 195, 210). He fills in the textual gaps with a name. He erects castration into *the* meaning of the text, its ultimate signified. In so doing, however, he makes the idea of castration itself into a readerly fetish, the supposed answer to all the text's questions, the final revelation in the "hermeneutic" code. Balzac indeed shows that the answer cannot be this simple, not only by eliminating the word *castration* from his text but also by suppressing the name of its opposite. When Sarrasine first feels sexual pleasure, Balzac says that this pleasure is located in "what we call the heart, for lack of any other word" (p. 238). Later Zambinella says "I have no heart" (p. 247). Barthes immediately calls "heart" a euphemism for the sexual organ, but Balzac's text, in stating that what the heart represents cannot be named, that the word is lacking, leaves the question of sexuality open, as a rhetorical problem which the simple naming of parts cannot solve. Balzac's text thus does not simply reverse the hierarchy between readerly and writerly by substituting the truth of castration for the delusion of wholeness; it deconstructs the very possibility of naming the difference.

On the basis of this confrontation between a literary and a critical text, we could perhaps conclude that while both involve a study of difference, the literary text conveys a difference from itself which it "knows" but cannot say, while the critical text, in attempting to say the difference, reduces it to identity. But in the final analysis, Barthes's text, too, displays a strange ambivalence. For although every metaphorical dimension in Barthes's text proclaims castration as the desirable essence of the writerly—the writerly about which "there may be nothing to say" (p. 4) just as the castrato is one "about whom there is nothing to say" (p. 214)—the literal concept of castration is loudly disavowed by Barthes as belonging to the injustices of the readerly: "To reduce the text to the unity of meaning, by a deceptively univocal reading, is . . . to sketch the castrating gesture" (p. 160). By means of this split, Barthes's own text reveals that it, like Balzac's, cannot with impunity set up any unequivocal value in opposition to the value of unequivocality. Just as Balzac's text, in its demystification of idealized beauty, reveals a difference not between the readerly and the writerly, but within the very ideals of the readerly, Barthes's text, in its ambivalence toward castration, reveals that the other of the readerly cannot but be subject to its own difference from itself. Difference as such cannot ever be affirmed as an ultimate value because it is that which subverts the very foundations of any affirmation of value. Castration can neither be assumed nor denied, but only enacted in the return of unsituable difference in every text. And the difference between literature and criticism consists perhaps only in the fact that criticism is more likely to be blind to the way in which its own critical difference from itself makes it, in the final analysis, literary.

2. Allegory's Trip-Tease:
The White Waterlily

If human beings were not divided into two biological sexes, there would probably be no need for literature. And if literature could truly say what the relations between the sexes are, we would doubtless not need much of it then, either. Somehow, however, it is not simply a question of literature's ability to say or not to say the truth of sexuality. For from the moment literature begins to try to set things straight on that score, literature itself becomes inextricable from the sexuality it seeks to comprehend. It is not the life of sexuality that literature cannot capture; it is literature that inhabits the very heart of what makes sexuality problematic for us speaking animals. Literature is not only a thwarted investigator but also an incorrigible perpetrator of the problem of sexuality.

In an effort to catch literature in the act of seducing sexuality away from what we thereby think is literality, I have chosen to analyze a prose poem by Mallarmé called *Le Nénuphar blanc* (*The White Waterlily*). The poem tells the story of nothing happening between a man in a rowboat and an unknown woman who may or may not be standing on the bank. The rower, whose boat has run into a tuft of reeds at the edge of the lady's property, hears an imperceptible noise, perhaps of footsteps, and ducks down deeper into his boat, all the while evoking to himself the flowing skirts of a feminine possibility. After a pause during which he does not determine whether or not anyone is actually present, he turns the boat around and, imagining himself carrying off a white waterlily, quietly rows away.

Far from lamenting this lack of action, Mallarmé's narrator pauses at the very climax of indeterminacy to generalize it as a superior form of intimacy:

13

Séparés, on est ensemble: je m'immisce à de sa confuse intimité, dans ce suspens sur l'eau où mon songe attarde l'indécise, mieux que visite, suivie d'autres,
l'autorisera. Que de discours oiseux en comparaison de celui que je tins pour
n'être pas entendu, faudra-t-il, avant de retrouver aussi intuitif accord que
maintenant. . .[1]

[Separated, one is together: I immerse myself in her confused intimacy, in that
suspense upon the water where my dream lets the indecisive one linger, better
than a visit followed by others would authorize. What a lot of idle discourse
compared to the speech I hold to be not heard would be necessary before re-
gaining such an intuitive accord as now. . .]

This has often been read as a statement of preference for the imaginary over the real, or for the idealized aesthetic image of femininity
over the banality of ordinary social or sexual intercourse. It is my aim
here to show that while this is indeed the tradition on which Mallarmé
is playing, this poem does not quite espouse such views, but rather
repeats them in order to analyze and question the very nature of the
relations between literature and sexuality.

The aesthetic tendency to overvalue the nonattainment of literal
sexual goals has a long and impressive history in Western literature,
occurring in the service both of the titillations and frustrations of deferment and of the promotion of higher spiritual values of which the
life of the body gives only a crude material image. This is particularly
true of allegorical literature, of which *Le Roman de la Rose* (*The
Romance of the Rose*) can here be considered exemplary, since the
history of its interpretations ("la querelle") is an oscillation between
delightful deferment and divine transfiguration.

Mallarmé situates his waterlily in the allegorical wake of the rose in
several explicit ways. Indeed, perhaps Mallarmé's role in literary history
could be summed up simply in his change of the flower's color from red
to white, or even to blank ("blanc"). Both texts make playful use of
the romance quest structure in the service of the plucking or nonpluck-
ing of the flower of femininity. In the *Roman de la Rose,* the dreamer's
task is to slip through a succession of obstacles and disarm the personified guardians that protect the rose like a medieval fortress. In Guillaume de Lorris's telling of the story, the dreamer never reaches the
rose, and it can be argued that this suspended ending is an inherent
necessity in the text rather than a mere accident of Guillaume's biogra-
phy. In Mallarmé's poem, the narrator refers to himself as an explorer
or aquatic marauder setting off on an adventure in which he must
reconnoiter the property of an unknown lady, eventually to return
with an imaginary trophy, the waterlily, from a battle of the sexes that
has not taken place. The poem ends in a volley of personifications of
the woman who has not been seen:

Si, attirée par un sentiment d'insolite, elle a paru, la Méditative ou la Hautaine, la Farouche, la Gaie, tant pis pour cette indicible mine que j'ignore à jamais!

[If, drawn by a sense of something out of the ordinary, she ever appeared, Miss Meditative, Dame Haughty, Mistress Skittish, Lady Gay, so much the worse for that ineffable face of which I am forever ignorant!]

The text then goes on:

car j'accomplis selon les règles la manoeuvre. . . .

[For I am completing the maneuver according to the rules. . . .]

On a first level, this statement is about the rower's maneuver in turning his boat around. But coming as it does between the four capitalized personifications and the final description of the carrying off of the imaginary trophy, the sentence can also be read as a reference to the rules of a *literary* maneuver, the rules of allegory that dictate that the lover's trophy be only a trope. The poet here does what is expected of him as a poet, contenting himself with a flower of rhetoric enclosing "un rien, fait de songes intacts, du bonheur qui n'aura pas lieu" ("a nothing, made of intact dreams, of the happiness that will not take place"). In this way the text marks its kinship with the tradition that holds that the literary maneuver as such involves a rhetorical displacement or circumvention of literal sexuality.

In order to follow Mallarmé's questioning of this opposition between trope and possession, between the figurative and the *propre,* we will go back to another similarity between *Le Roman de la Rose* and *Le Nénuphar blanc:* the centrality of the reflecting pool or narcissistic mirror whose function in both texts is to trigger the erotic desire. In the *Roman de la Rose,* the dreamer approaches a fountain explicitly labeled as the spot where Narcissus died, and it is there reflected in the water that he first sees the rose he elects as his beloved. In *Le Nénuphar,* the narrator begins to become interested in the lady when he identifies the watery park as hers:

Un joli voisinage, pendant la saison, la nature d'une personne qui s'est choisi retraite aussi humidement impénétrable ne pouvant être que conforme à mon goût. Sûr, elle avait fait de ce cristal son miroir intérieur. . . .

[A pretty neighborhood, for the season, the nature of a person that would choose such a humidly impenetrable retreat being quite in conformity with my taste. It is sure that she had made this crystal place into her own inner mirror. . . .]

It can be said that each of these flower stories takes up where the Narcissus myth leaves off, since Narcissus himself, after his death, is transformed into a flower. Physically, however, the white waterlily, which is compared to a swan's egg from which no flight will ever spring, is itself the exact inverted mirror image of the lady:

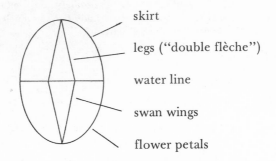

skirt

legs ("double flèche")

water line

swan wings

flower petals

The rowboat with its two oars can also be seen as the inverted image of the lady, so that the white waterlily becomes a metaphor not only of the woman but also of the man, while the man in turn becomes the narcissistic reflection of the woman.[2]

The function of the mirror here is thus not only to duplicate but also to reverse: the lady reflected in the water is upside down. If we take into account what Freud says about the inversion of a detail in a dream—and Mallarmé apostrophizes his experience as a dream—we might now ask whether this reversal has any more general analogues in the rest of the text. First, the place of the man and the woman are reversed with respect to the story of Echo and Narcissus—here it is the woman who reflects herself in the pool and the man who watches impotently. Or again, what is reflected of the lady is invisible, while the discourse of the man is held "pour n'être pas entendu." In other words, the original relation between image and echo has become a relation between the blank and the silent.

But on a more general level, the allegory itself seems somehow upside down in comparison with its traditional structure. Normally, allegory presents a narrative of concrete events which, upon interpretation, yields a second narrative that is figurative and abstract. But here, an abstract nothing occurs on the literal level ("Rien n'aura eu lieu que le lieu"), while a concrete sexual description is being fleshed out on the figurative level of the poem. The boatman traveling up the wet canal stops at a tuft of reeds where he can spy a "retraite humidement impénétrable," which is a "miroir intérieur" of a lady seeking privacy. But he never sees or does anything concrete. He positions himself at a vantage point from which he can merge with a certain imagined "charme instinctif d'en dessous" ("instinctive charm from underneath"). When withdrawing from her intimacy, he does not actually even pluck the waterlily but imagines himself doing so by analogy, deflowering the "vierge absence éparse" ("scattered virgin absence") and fleeing with the hope that he has not left behind any "ressemblance transparente du rapt de mon idéale fleur" ("transparent likeness to the ravishing of my ideal flower").

The pleasure afforded by this poem is thus produced by the tension between the nothing that happens literally and the sexual act that is mapped out figuratively. The key sentence of the text, "Séparés, on est ensemble," can thus be seen as a description of this very functioning of allegory itself. The figurative description is so suggestive that the reader inevitably thinks he has seen a man peering under the skirts of a woman oblivious of his presence, whereas it is actually the woman whose presence is purely hypothetical.

But is the poem simply saying that the trip was the equivalent of a sexual act? Or is it saying something different about all close encounters of an erotic kind? Since both levels of the text are so fully perceptible, and since their *not* merging is what gives the reader pleasure, it might be fruitful to consider the very discrepancy between happening and not happening, absence and intimacy, possession and impenetrability, literality and rhetoric, as the first level of a more complex allegorical structure. The poem would not then be saying one thing by means of another, but would instead be putting forth discrepancy and division as its essential message. Neither on the allegorical level nor on the interpersonal level are we ever quite certain whether one thing is not really two, or two one. Looking again at that crucial sentence, we find it loaded with numerical ambiguity:

Séparés, on est ensemble: je m'immisce à de sa confuse intimité. . .

The adjective "séparés," for example, is plural in form and yet designates isolation. The word "on" is singular and impersonal where one would expect *nous,* personal and plural. The subject and verb of the first part of the sentence are thus singular and universal in a context of private coupledom. "Ensemble," too, is an adjective that is always singular in form and plural in meaning. In the second part of the passage quoted, "je m[e]" finally provides us with the personal pronoun but immediately divides the subject into two halves. And "m'immisce" and "confuse" both designate heterogeneous substances no longer numerically extricable from each other. In sum, in "Séparés, on est ensemble," it is as though $2 = 1$; in "je m'immisce à de sa confuse intimité," it is as though $1 = 2 \rightarrow \infty$. The precondition of togetherness seems to be separation, while the act of merging with the other divides the subject in two.

Division is also present in the originating moment of the erotic impulse, when the lady becomes appealing because she is imagined doubled by her reflection. It is thus precisely the functioning of discrepancies of levels and permutations of numbers that characterizes the erotic. At the same time, the act of reading this constant shifting between separation and confusion, projection and interruption, implicitly itself becomes an erotic experience. In both cases, a structure that is supposed to involve the creation of a complementary union between two separate terms—man and woman, text and interpretation—becomes, rather, a structure in which the initial separability of the two terms cannot be taken for granted, while at the same time the unity of each individual term consists in its infinite capacity for division. It would seem that the margin between an object's simple (meaningless) existence and its acquisition of erotic or rhetorical significance involves its becoming somehow more or less than the context requires. The mirror image, which imbues the lady with erotic potential, will also make any real possession of what is thereby desired impossible.

The poem is thus dramatizing sexuality as a rhythm of multiplications, divisions, and fusions, a series of trespassings over the bounds of unity or property, an appearance and disappearance of partition. Divisions, thresholds, veils, boundary lines are ubiquitous, so that a flickering of exposures and concealments, transgressions and interdictions, ends up installing the *fact* of division, the functioning of rhythm, as the ultimate referent of the allegorical trip-tease.

That Mallarmé's poetry has as its aim not the revelation of truth, nudity, or ideality but the dynamic dramatization of the rhythm of pure difference is attested both by his explicit statements and by his syntactic practices.[3] This does not mean that his poetry is empty of meaning, but that it works to catch difference and division in the act of both producing and subverting significance as such. Consider, for example, the number of ways in which he represents something like the bar separating the conscious from the unconscious, or, using the Lacanian interpretation of the Saussurian sign—S/s—, the dividing line between the signifier and the (repressed) signified.[4] To take an example from a quite different context: on the face of a worldly spectator incapable of understanding the theatrical spectacle he is attending, Mallarmé sees "la barre de favoris couper d'ombre une joue comme par un *Ce n'est pas moi dont il est question*" ("the bar of sideburns cutting the cheek with shadow as if saying *It is not me that is in question*") (p. 315). Another example is found when in the following well-known sentence in the *Hamlet* article one places the emphasis on the word *rampe* (footlights):

Son solitaire drame! et qui, parfois, tant ce promeneur d'un labyrinthe de
trouble et de griefs en prolonge les circuits avec le suspens d'un acte inachevé,
semble le spectacle même pourquoi existent la rampe ainsi que l'espace doré
quasi moral qu'elle défend, car il n'est point d'autre sujet, sachez bien: l'an-
tagonisme de rêve chez l'homme avec les fatalités à son existence départies par
le malheur. (P. 300)

[His solitary drama! and which, at times—so much does this stroller through a
labyrinth of troubles and grievances prolong its circuits through the suspense of
an unaccomplished act—seems to be the very spectacle for which the footlights
were made, along with the golden quasi-moral space they defend, for there is
no other subject, mark this well: the dream antagonism in man toward the
fated events meted out through his existence by misfortune.]

This is not only a lament for lost dreams of happiness; it is also a
description of the irreducibility of man's *départition,* which is superbly
represented by the *rampe*'s division of the theater into a golden conscious stage and a dark populous house.

In *Le Nénuphar blanc,* it is the lady's belt that serves to divide her in
two, the head or visage being the worldly conscious self and the part
below the belt representing a "charme *instinctif* d'en dessous (emphasis
mine)." That this can be considered the signified is indicated by the expressions "vague concept" and "délice empreint de généralité." But
here it is consciousness, the woman's face, that the poet wishes to
repress:

Si vague concept se suffit: et ne transgressera le délice empreint de généralité
qui permet et ordonne d'exclure tous visages, au point que la révélation d'un
(n'allez point le pencher, avéré, sur le furtif seuil où je règne) chasserait mon
trouble, avec lequel il n'a que faire.

[So vague a concept suffices: and will not transgress the delight imbued with
generality that allows and demands that all faces be excluded, to the point that
the revelation of one (do not go bending it down, avowedly, over the furtive
threshold where I reign) would chase away my confused arousal, with which it
has nothing to do.]

To become one with the other's unconscious without negotiating
through the divisions and contradictions produced when the conscious,
worldly, conversational head is included can only be a fragile, unauthor-
ized, fantasmatic act on a "furtive threshold." The "intuitive accord"
achieved between the narrator and the *indécise*—the undivided—whom
he suspends over the water of his fantasy can only be "a nothing, made
of intact dreams, of the happiness that will not take place." Any more
real togetherness would necessarily jangle this "intuitive accord" since
it would have to involve the embrace of the other's division. Then, too,

the poet's parenthetical command not to bend too closely over the furtive threshold on which he reigns can be read as an admonition to the *reader*, a warning that it is the furtiveness of the threshold itself, not what lies beyond it, that constitutes what the text avows. Division, contradiction, incompatibility, and ellipsis thus stand as the challenge, the enigma, the despair, and the delight both of the lover and of the reader of literature.

PART TWO:
POETRY
AND DIFFERENCE

3. Poetry and Its Double:
Two *Invitations au voyage*

Poetic Cookery

> Mange-t-on dans *René*?
>> —Balzac, *Falthurne*

> On mange beaucoup dans les romans de Flaubert.
>> —Jean-Pierre Richard, *Littérature et Sensation*

The prose version of Baudelaire's *Invitation au voyage* appeared in 1857, two years after its well-known homonym in verse.[1] It did not, however, meet with the same success; already transported by the rhythmic precision and calm lyricism of the versified text, readers of the prose poem have always tended to decline its invitation. Their refusal, varying from regrets to indignation, generally takes the form of a comparison, devaluing the prose in favor of the verse. For example, the *Invitation* in prose, writes Jacques Crépet, "sounds infinitely less pure and less musical: it is weighed down by moral and practical considerations which drag it either toward the exposition of ideas or toward everyday reality."[2] And Suzanne Bernard, after juxtaposing the verse poem's refrain—

> Là, tout n'est qu'ordre et beauté,
> Luxe, calme et volupté—

> [There, all is but order and beauty,
> Luxury, calm, and sensual pleasure.]

with the prose description of a "pays de Cocagne,"

> où le luxe a plaisir à se mirer dans l'ordre; où la vie est grasse et douce à respirer; d'où le désordre, la turbulence et l'imprévu sont exclus; où le bonheur est

23

marié au silence; où la cuisine elle-même est poétique, grasse et excitante à la fois . . . ,

[where luxury is pleased to mirror itself in order; where life is rich and sweet to breathe; where disorder, turmoil, and the unforeseen are excluded; where happiness is married to silence; where the cooking itself is poetic, rich and stimulating at once . . . ,]

exclaims, "What! all *that* was in Baudelaire's dream of voluptuous beauty! A quiet, comfortable life with 'rich and stimulating' food!"[3]

In the act of refusing the invitation into prose, these readers thus accept with a vengeance Baudelaire's invitation to compare. And their verdict is generally the same: what is wrong with the prose lies in what it adds to the imagery of the verse. The new elements are considered discordant, extraneous, and unpoetic. For these readers, then, every plus in the prose poem is a minus.

For a small minority of readers, on the other hand, it is the very heterogeneity of the prose poem's imagery which heightens its poetic effect: "In the *Invitation au voyage* . . . seduction and tenderness reach their peak in metaphors which unite abstract feelings with the most prosaic objects of the culinary arts."[4]

But however radical the divergence between these two ways of judging the prose poem, their agreement over the element, namely, cooking, to valorize or to condemn is striking. Considered either as a lapse in taste or as a new stylistic spice, the unexpected presence of these culinary images within a "poetic" text has always given rise to the same question, Can cooking really be poetic? This, however, is precisely the question the text does not allow us to ask, since it has already answered: Cooking itself is poetic. Rather than the status of the word *cooking,* it is the status of the word *poetic* that is at stake. What must be asked is thus not Can cooking be poetic? but What does *poetic* mean? Because the prose version of Baudelaire's *Invitation au voyage* gives an affirmative answer to the first question, it renews the urgency and uncertainty of the second.

If the text's own use of the word *poetic* in a culinary context is rejected by certain readers, it can only be in function of a conception of poetry derived from somewhere else. In Suzanne Bernard's case, this conception comes from certain statements made by Baudelaire in his article on Banville:

The lyre gladly flees all the details on which the novel feasts. The lyric soul strides as wide as a synthesis; the mind of the novelist regales itself with analysis.[5]

For Bernard, then, *poetic* = *lyric,* and lyric poetry is no place for the kitchen. Baudelaire's distinction between the lyrical and the novelistic parallels the distinction suggested by our two epigraphs between the "lyrical" prose of Chateaubriand and the "realistic" prose of Flaubert: the presence or absence of the act of eating in the two works illustrates the Baudelairian distinction between the presence or absence of "detail"; "eating" in a text thereby takes on the status of an index to the text's genre.

Bernard's inability to swallow the "rich, stimulating food" in the prose *Invitation* thus results not from a simple excess of detail but from a conflict of codes. Cooking, which is certainly foreign to the lyric tradition, here disturbs the coherence of the poetic code—but it does so in order to reveal that the "poetic" is itself nothing but a code. Baudelaire indeed investigates the way poetry functions *as* a code in the prose *Invitation,* as well as in many other prose poems. The fact that many readers find the genre of the *Petits poèmes en prose* problematic is due to what might be called a "code struggle" going on both between the verse and the prose poems and within the individual prose poems themselves.[6]

If the mention of cooking in the prose *Invitation* thus represents the intrusion of a novelistic or realistic code in a poetic context—and we still of course do not know what "poetic" means—what is it that, within this so-called code struggle, can be said to represent the "lyric" code? Let us take another look at Baudelaire's distinction.

> The lyre gladly flees all the details on which the novel feasts. The lyric soul strides as wide as a synthesis; the mind of the novelist regales itself with analysis.

Curiously enough, the close relation between novels, details, and food is suggested here not only in the meaning of Baudelaire's statement, but also in its very terms, in the figurative use of the verbs *feast* and *regale* (se régaler, se délecter) to describe the work of the novelist. And while the verbs associated with novels thus evoke a kind of metabolic incorporation, the verbs associated with lyricism are rather verbs of hyperbolic motion (*flee, stride*): the delights of dining give way, in the lyric, to the pleasures of traveling. The lyric, in other words, turns out to be nothing other than a kind of *voyage*.

The Rhetorical Voyage

> Il n'y a rien qu'on puisse appeler langage avant l'articulation, c'est-à-dire la différence locale. . . . La société, la langue, l'histoire, l'articulation . . . naissent . . . en même temps que la prohibition de l'inceste.
>
> —Derrida, *De la grammatologie*

It is clear that a major participant in the prose *Invitation*'s code struggle will be the text of the *Invitation* in verse, the lyric voyage par excellence in Baudelaire's work. Let us therefore begin by analyzing the nature of the lyrical invitation presented in that poem:

> Mon enfant, ma soeur,
> Songe à la douceur
> D'aller là-bas vivre ensemble!
> Aimer à loisir,
> Aimer et mourir
> Au pays qui te ressemble!

[My child, my sister,/Dream of the sweetness/Of going there to live together!/ To love at leisure/To love and die/In the land that resembles you!]

In inviting his lady to the "land that resembles" her, the poem's speaker begins not with a description of the land but with an affirmation of its metaphorical status. What is being proposed to the woman is a place created in her own image, a place toward which she would stand in necessary and symmetrical relation, a place, in other words, that would serve as her mirror. And indeed, the word *mirror* does appear in the very center of the poem. The lyric voyage, then, is a voyage through the looking-glass, a voyage into the illusory "depths" ("les miroirs *profonds*" [emphasis mine here and passim]) of a reflection. Its desired end is the perfect metaphorical union of the *destinatrice* with the *destination*.

Grammatically, however, this seemingly transparent metaphorical specularity is not so simple. In speaking of the relation between the lady and the land as a relation of perfectly symmetrical duality, we have not taken into account the dialogical status of the metaphorical affirmation. But it is precisely at the point at which the speaker seems to describe the metaphor in terms of the most objectively referential, visual resemblance between lady and land that its mediation through a third focal point becomes explicit:

> Les soleils mouillés
> De ces ciels brouillés
> *Pour mon esprit ont les charmes*
> Si mystérieux
> De tes traîtres yeux
> Brillant à travers leurs larmes.

[The watery suns/In these misty skies/*For my spirit have the very charm*/ Which is so mysterious/Of your treacherous eyes/Shining through their tears.]

The important common denominator between land and lady, between suns and eyes, is less their shared shining roundness than a common

effect produced on the "spirit" of the beholder. The rhetorical meeting
point between the two terms (eyes and suns) is not simply that of a
metaphorical resemblance but that of a metonymical third term, contiguous to both: the speaker's desire. Metaphor, in other words, is the
effect, not the cause, of the metonymy of desire.

There is yet another problem in the seemingly transparent, referential grounding of the metaphor. For if metaphor consists, as Fontanier
puts it, "in presenting one idea under the sign of another idea which is
more striking or better known,"[7] what is it that here stands as the
"better known" point of comparison, if not, paradoxically, a woman
whose charms are mysterious and whose eyes are treacherous—a woman,
in other words, who is quite unknown, and perhaps unknowable? The
"you" that serves as the point of reference ("the land that resembles
you") is itself the unknown in the equation. And the land where "all
is but order and beauty, luxury, calm, and sensual pleasure" is not in
reality a land that is just like the lady, but a description of what the
speaker wishes the lady were like.

It is thus metaphor itself that has become an "Invitation to the
Voyage," a process of seduction. And if, as the abbé du Bos puts it,
poetry can be called "l'art d'émouvoir les hommes et de les amener
où l'on veut" ("the art of moving men and leading them wherever
one likes"), then this metaphorical seduction, this poetic voyage, does
not consist of moving in space but of moving the desires of a person.

Let us examine the nature of this rhetorical operation more closely.
In the opening invocation, "Mon enfant, ma soeur," familiarity coincides with familiality; the desired union between two contiguous beings
("vivre ensemble") is placed under the natural sign of genetic resemblance. The metonymic meeting between two separate subjects takes
place within a metaphorical bond of biological likeness. And if such a
union is by definition incestuous, then incest becomes, in rhetorical
terms, the perfect convergence of metaphor and metonymy.

The same convergence can in fact be seen in the relation between
the lady and the land; while a person's relation to place is by definition
metonymic, that is, arbitrary and contingent, here it is said to be
metaphorical, that is, motivated and symmetrical. Metaphor thus becomes a process both of writing—the writing of resemblance—and of
erasing—the erasing of difference. And the difference it erases is not
only that between person and place; it is nothing less than the difference between metaphor and metonymy as such. If the entire field of
language is described as the space engendered by the two axes of
metaphor and metonymy[8]—that is, by their separation—the rhetoric
of Baudelaire's *Invitation au voyage* would thus seem to be situated

entirely at the intersection of the two axes, at the point which, in mathematical parlance, is called the *origin*.

Interestingly enough, the poem leads us toward this "origin" of language:

> Tout y parlerait
> A l'âme en secret
> Sa douce *langue natale*.

[There, all would speak/To the soul in secret/Its sweet *native language*.]

This evocation of a first, original language makes of the voyage not a departure but a return, the erasing of the distance covered by a previous voyage, the elimination of the interval that separates the "soul" from its origin. Again, we rejoin Baudelaire's remarks about lyricism: "Any lyric poet, by his very nature, inevitably brings about a return toward the lost Eden."[9] Origin, Eden, incest: through the process of obliteration of all difference—spatial, temporal, linguistic, or intersubjective— the voyage seems to tend toward a primal fullness, immobile and undifferentiated, prior to movement, time, and law. This Edenic state of perfection indeed constitutes itself through the exclusion of imperfection, as its privative grammar indicates: "Tout *n'est que* . . ." Each one of the abstract nouns following the "All is but . . ." seems to name —all by itself—the totality of the "all"; paradoxically, the "all" is not equal to the sum of its parts; rather, it is the elimination of all partition.

Ultimately, however, this suppression of all difference, division, or distance can only result in a tautology without syntax, that is, in the abolition of language as an articulated space structured by differences. And just as the origin of a mathematical graph is the point at which all variables are equal to zero, this elimination of all variation or difference in language, this Edenic point of primal fullness, can only be a u-topia, a dimensionless point, a nonplace. The poetic "native language," the origin of signification, the convergence of metaphor and metonymy, in reality marks nothing less than the disappearance of language as such.

How then can we situate the language of this text with respect to the silence that is its origin and end? How does the text *say* the end of the voyage if the end of the voyage is an absence of text? Let us look at the poem's last stanza:

> Vois sur ces canaux
> Dormir ces vaisseaux
> Dont l'humeur est vagabonde;
> C'est pour assouvir
> Ton moindre désir
> Qu'ils viennent du bout du monde.

—Les soleils couchants
Revêtent les champs,
Les canaux, la ville entière,
D'hyacinthe et d'or;
Le monde s'endort
Dans une chaude lumière.

[See on these canals/These ships sleeping/In vagabond spirit/It is to fulfill/
Your least desire/That they come from the ends of the earth./—The setting
suns/Clothe the fields,/The canals, the entire town,/In hyacinth and gold;/
The world falls asleep/In a warm light.]

Are these ships, which "come from the ends of the earth" to "fulfill
your least desire," in the process of leaving or arriving? In spite of the
demonstratives ("*ces* canaux," "*ces* vaisseaux") and the present tenses
("ils viennent," "le monde s'endort"), the trip's end-point seems
curiously missing. More curiously still, this eclipse of the end is inscribed as such in the text, by the use of a dash ("—Les soleils couchants"), which both opens up and deletes, within the very space of
language, the locus of the end—of ecstasy or death. Indeed, the silence
of the end is in no way an end; it is but a stroke of the pen, deferring
for a moment what follows. If the poem's language is thus organized
around its own disappearance, that disappearance turns out to be not
an asymptotic limit external to the text—its end or origin—but its own
necessary and inherent discontinuity, the very principle of its spacing,
its articulation, and its rhythm.

Declining the Invitation

Cette fois, on sent l'effort dans ce système allégorique—qui remplace le tableau
lumineux et calme évoqué à la fin du poème en vers.
                              —Suzanne Bernard, *Le Poème en prose de Baudelaire à nos jours.*

As we have just seen, the lyrical invitation operates on two levels
which are traditionally called *rhetorical:* the level of *persuasion* (seduction) and the level of *figure* (convergence of metaphor and metonymy).
In both cases, the poem tends toward the transformation of all plurality
and difference into unity and sameness. In contrast, the rhetoric of the
prose *Invitation au voyage* is, from its very first sentence, quite different:

Il est un pays superbe, un pays de Cocagne, dit-on, que je rêve de visiter avec
une vieille amie.

[There is a superb country, a land of Cockaigne, they say, which I dream of
visiting with an old friend.]

Contrary to the incestuous intimacy and shared dream of the verse poem, the prose poem begins not only without invocation but also without interlocution. The lady is not at first addressed directly by the text, but is inscribed within the text in the third person ("une vieille amie"): she has become, in Benveniste's terms, not a person but a non-person,[10] a grammatical instance designating her absence instead of her presence. This grammatical change in the invitation—which is thus no longer a real invitation—subverts the intimacy between "I" and "you" which, in the verse poem, had led to an Edenic "us" ("notre chambre") in which each could find in the other, transformed into the same, the essence of his own soul. Between the "I" and the "old friend," no direct seduction can take place: speaking *to* has become speaking *of.* The lady is depersonalized into a mere social role, the role of the "old friend," or, later, of the "chosen sister" ("soeur d'élection")—an expression that unmasks the entirely arbitrary, conventional character of the lyric invocation "my child, my sister." As a social stereotype, the lady in the prose poem changes from the unique object of an incestuous love to the locus of an infinite possibility of substitution.

In the same way, the usage of the third person subverts the originality and uniqueness of the speaker himself. The dream is announced from the very beginning as belonging to the language of others: "Il est un pays superbe, un pays de Cocagne, dit-on . . . " The real author of this dream is not "I" but "they"; the dreamer dreams by hearsay, as part of the repertoire of social rites to which the sending of any invitation—or even any love poem—ultimately belongs.

Having thus begun by subverting the immediacy of the dialogue between the first and second persons by the constant intrusion of the third, the prose poem nevertheless goes on to make abundant use of the first and second person pronouns, which had in fact never appeared as grammatical subjects in the verse poem. Interlocution, which was absent from the opening lines of the prose poem, returns with a vengeance. It would thus seem that in conserving the I/you dialogue within a context that questions its very conditions of possibility, the prose poem is situating *its* dialogue not between the first and second persons, but between the function of person (*je, tu*) and the function of non-person (*elle, on*), between the lyric illusion of dialogic reciprocity and symmetry and the ironic asymmetry that disrupts and displaces that illusion.

While the prose poem thus puts in question the specular symmetry between the "I" and the "you," it nonetheless seems to accentuate and elaborate on the specular symmetry between the land and the lady:

Un vrai pays de Cocagne . . . où tout vous ressemble . . . . Il est une contrée qui te ressemble . . . Fleur incomparable, tulipe retrouvée, allégorique dahlia . . .

ne serais-tu pas encadrée dans ton analogie, et ne pourrais-tu pas te mirer, pour parler comme les mystiques, dans ta propre *correspondance?*. . . Vivrons-nous jamais, passerons-nous jamais dans ce tableau qu'a peint mon esprit, ce tableau qui te ressemble? . . . Ces trésors, ces meubles, ce luxe, cet ordre, ces parfums, ces fleurs miraculeuses, c'est toi. C'est encore toi, ces grands fleuves et ces canaux tranquilles. . . . (Emphasis in original)

[A veritable land of Cockaigne . . . where everything resembles you. . . . There is a land which resembles you . . . . Incomparable flower, rediscovered tulip, allegorical dahlia . . . wouldn't you be framed by your analogy, and couldn't you, to speak like the mystics, mirror yourself in your own *correspondence?* . . . Shall we ever live, shall we ever pass into this picture my mind has painted, this painting that resembles you? . . . These treasures, these furnishings, this luxury, this order, these perfumes, these miraculous flowers, are all you. So are these rivers and tranquil canals. . . .]

The notion of "correspondences" mentioned in the poem embodies a conception of metaphor which was in fact an artistic commonplace in Baudelaire's day. From Swedenborg to Madame de Staël, from Schelling to the abbé Constant, the idea of correspondences served not only to account for "analogies among the different elements of physical nature" but also to reveal "the supreme law of creation, the variety in unity and the unity in variety."[11] In other words, metaphor was a proof of the existence of God:

All things in nature from the smallest to the largest are but so many correspondences, for the natural world exists and conserves itself through the spiritual world, and both of them through the Lord.[12]

In Baudelaire's prose poem, the planting of the "flower" in a land comparable to it, the land of its "own correspondence," seems designed to insure both the stability of the flower's identity (its likeness to itself) and the unity and order of the whole poetic universe. If this flower is said to be, paradoxically, an *"incomparable* flower," if it is defined, in other words, as at once incomparable and comparable, being both what founds and what transcends the poem's system of comparisons, then the flower is indeed, like God, what can be likened to everything without ceasing to be unique. Metaphor here turns out to be a process of obliteration of the inherent contradiction between substitution (the comparable) and the unique (the incomparable).

Baudelaire, however, refers to the notion of correspondences not only so as "to speak like the mystics" but also so as to speak like—and comment on—another Baudelaire, the Baudelaire who wrote a sonnet called *Correspondances*. In that sonnet, the word *comme* (like)—used seven times in fourteen lines—acts as a kind of "Archimedes' fulcrum"[13] to lift up the "ténébreuse et profonde unité" ("deep, dark unity") of the world. Now, in our prose poem, the word *comme* occurs ten times, reaching an apotheosis in the following lines:

> Un vrai pays de Cocagne, te dis-je, où tout est riche, propre et luisant, *comme* une belle conscience, *comme* une magnifique batterie de cuisine, *comme* une splendide orfèvrerie, *comme* une bijouterie bariolée!

> [A veritable land of Cockaigne, I tell you, where all is rich, clean and shiny, *like* a clear conscience, *like* a magnificent set of cookware, *like* the splendid wares of a goldsmith, *like* a gaudy set of jewelry!]

But here, instead of conveying a "deep, dark unity," the word *comme*—bringing with it, as we have seen, a code struggle, a conflict of codes—conveys a nonunified, heterogeneous plurality. In pushing *ad absurdum* the possibility of comparison, the prose poem transforms the word *like* from a necessary link in the world's order to a mere linguistic reflex, conventional and arbitrary. This ironic proliferation of likenesses does not render comparison impossible, but it does put in question the validity of taking comparison as a sign of the ultimate unity of the world.

In the same way, the lady to whom "all" is compared has become such a miscellaneous collection of objects ("treasures," "furniture," "luxury," "perfumes," "rivers," "canals") that she is finally nothing but that to which *anything* can be compared: this "allegorical flower" is no longer the point of primal convergence, of metaphorical fusion, where metaphor and metonymy, signified and signifier, harmoniously unite, but the very locus of substitution and of dissemination, a mere linguistic constant in an infinitely extensible equation.

Just as this allegorical flower has been rhetorically emptied of any reliable identity through the mechanical proliferation of its likenesses, so too the lyrical "soul"—central to the verse poem's inner voyage ("tout y parlerait/A l'âme en secret/Sa douce langue natale")—here undergoes a parallel transformation. In affirming that "tu les conduis [mes pensées] doucement vers la mer qui est l'Infini, *tout en réfléchissant les profondeurs du ciel dans la limpidité de ta belle âme*" ("you lead my thoughts gently toward the sea which is the Infinite, while *reflecting the depths of the heavens in the limpidity of your beautiful soul*"), the poet has transformed the very "depths" of the soul into a mere specular illusion. The correspondence between heaven and earth has literally become a play of reflections, not between two depths or essences, but between two shining surfaces. The image of the shining surface is in fact ubiquitous in this poem:

> *Les miroirs*, les métaux, les étoffes, l'orfévrerie et la faience y jouent pour les yeux une symphonie muette . . . Un vrai pays de Cocagne, te dis-je, où *tout*

est riche, propre et luisant, comme une belle conscience, comme une magnifique batterie de cuisine, comme une splendide orfévrerie, comme une bijouterie bariolée!

[The mirrors, the metals, the cloth, the gold, and the crockery play for the
eyes a mute symphony . . .]

"Everything" in this imaginary land thus resembles a glistening mirror—
including the "conscience" (consciousness, or conscience). Ironically,
the "belle conscience" has here become, in a literal sense, what it is
often called in a figurative sense: the seat of reflection.

But if everything has become a mirror, then the normal function
of the mirror as a confirmation of identity has been uncannily subverted and infinitely *mise en abyme*. In the very terms in which he
invites the lady to the land of her own correspondence and offers her
an infinite reflection of her self, the poet in fact transforms that self
into an empty hall of mirrors: if the lady can mirror herself in what
resembles her ("ne pourrais-tu pas *te mirer* . . . dans ta propre correspondance?"), she is no longer seen *in* the mirror; she has become a
mirror herself. And if the lady's *"propre* correspondance" (her *"own*
correspondence") is simply a surface that is *"propre"* ("clean"), then
the *propriétés* (properties) that are supposed to constitute identity are
derived from mere *propreté* (cleanness). The two senses of the word
propre have curiously become interchangeable.

But questions of property and propriety do not stop here. For if
the conscience is as clean as a set of pots and pans, then it must itself
be part of a general and daily housecleaning, in which dishwashing and
brainwashing are somehow equivalent. This brings us to the strange
presence of moral and economic considerations in the text of the prose
Invitation.

Ethics, Economics, and Poetics

Je veux parler de l'hérésie de *l'enseignement,* laquelle comprend comme
corollaires inévitables l'hérésie de la *passion,* de la *vérité* et de la *morale.* . . .
La poésie ne peut pas, sous peine de mort ou de défaillance, s'assimiler à la
science ou à la morale; elle n'a pas la Vérité pour objet, elle n'a qu'Elle-même.

Baudelaire, *Notes nouvelles sur Edgar Poe*

"Il est une contrée qui te ressemble, où tout est beau, riche, tranquille et *honnête"* ("There is a country which resembles you, where all
is beautiful, rich, tranquil, and *honest"*). Appearing as it does in the
midst of an echo of the verse poem's refrain, the word *honest* is doubly
jolting: it breaks the repetition, and it introduces into the prose poem a

system of moral values totally foreign to the voluptuous amorality of the verse poem. Like cooking, honesty is the sign of the intrusion of a different code; it belongs to the literature of bourgeois morality against which Baudelaire often vituperated, and which seems to assert, as Baudelaire puts it, that "any honest man who knows how to please his wife is a sublime poet."[14] About Emile Augier's play *Gabrielle,* which received a prize for its morality, Baudelaire sneers:

> Listen to Gabrielle, virtuous Gabrielle, calculating with her virtuous husband how many years of virtuous avarice—with interest—it will take them to reach an income of ten or twenty thousand pounds. Five years, ten years . . . then, says this honest couple:
> WE CAN LIVE LIKE A WEALTHY PLAYBOY!
> . . . M. Augier . . . has spoken the language of shopkeepers . . . mistaking it for the language of virtue.[15]

But curiously enough, the language of commerce and avarice is also the language of the prose *Invitation:*

> Un vrai pays de Cocagne, te dis-je, où tout est *riche,* propre et luisant, comme une *belle conscience,* comme une magnifique *batterie de cuisine,* comme une splendide *orfèvrerie,* comme une *bijouterie* bariolée! Les *trésors* du monde y affluent, comme dans la maison d'un homme *laborieux* et qui a *bien mérité* du monde entier.
> . . . Ces énormes navires . . . tout chargés de *richesses* . . . ce sont mes pensées . . . . Tu les conduis doucement vers la mer qui est l'Infini . . . et quand, fatigués par la houle et *gorgés des produits de l'Orient,* ils rentrent au port natal, ce sont encore mes pensées *enrichies* qui reviennent de l'Infini vers toi.

> [A veritable land of Cockaigne, I tell you, where all is *rich,* clean, and shiny, like a *clear conscience,* like a magnificent *set of cookware,* like the splendid *wares of a goldsmith,* like a gaudy *set of jewelry!* The *treasures* of the earth abound there, as in the house of a *laborious* man to whom the whole world is *indebted* . . . . These enormous ships . . . loaded with *riches* . . . are my thoughts. . . . You lead them gently toward the sea which is the Infinite . . . and when, fatigued by the swell and *stuffed with products from the Orient,* they come back to their native port, they are still my thoughts, grown *richer,* which come back from the Infinite to you.]

This trip to the Orient seems more like a business affair than an affair of the heart. What is sought in this voyage is not love, but "riches." Honesty exists only to protect property; everything becomes a commodity, including the "clear conscience," as useful to the "laborious man" as his pots and pans. The land of Cockaigne is no longer a land of erotic fantasy, but an exploitable source of riches, a colony.

This unexpected appearance of "shopkeeper language" in a text of poetic imagination thus forces us to examine three fundamental notions that underlie the bourgeois system with which the prose poem allies itself: the notion of value, the notion of work, and the notion of economy.

In the verse poem, the word *luxury* seemed to refer to some vague poetic quality called "Oriental splendor," having nothing to do with questions of production or exchange. But the source of the "treasures," which "abound" in the prosaic land of Cockaigne, is explicitly located in the working man's labor: "les trésors du monde y affluent, *comme dans la maison d'un homme laborieux* et qui a bien *mérité* du monde entier." If the imaginary country's value ("richesse," "luxe," "trésors," etc.) here results from a correspondence ("mérite") between work and wages, then the aesthetic notion of correspondences takes on an *economic* meaning.

This similarity between poetics and economics reaches a climax at the end of the prose poem, where the ships ("my thoughts") go out "loaded with riches" and come back "stuffed with Oriental goods." What the sonnet *Correspondances* calls the "transports of spirit and sense" are here literalized, making the metaphorical voyage (etymologically, *metaphor* literally means "transport") into a business trip. The prose poem thus reveals that "poeticity" has its own economy, that the equating of signifier with signified, of the lady with the land, functions in the same way as the equating of wage with labor, or of product with price.

It is, however, precisely in *opposition* to the economy of exchange that the prose poem situates its ultimate object of desire:

> Qu'ils cherchent, qu'ils cherchent encore, qu'ils reculent sans cesse les limites de leur bonheur, ces alchimistes de l'horticulture! Qu'ils proposent des prix de soixante et de cent mille florins our qui résoudra leurs ambitieux problèmes! Moi, j'ai trouvé ma *tulipe noire* et mon *dahlia bleu!* (Emphasis in original)

> [Let them search, let them go on searching, let them push back forever the limits of their happiness, these alchemists of horticulture! Let them offer to pay sixty or a hundred thousand florins to anyone who can solve their ambitious problems! As for me, I have found my *black tulip* and my *blue dahlia!*]

It is this priceless, "incomparable" flower that, representing the highest poetic value, seems to locate the poetic universe somewhere beyond and above the economic sphere. This aesthetic transcendence of the structure of economic exchange is indeed a commonplace of traditional poetics:

> For a fine art must be free art in a double sense: i.e., not alone in a sense opposed to contract work, as not being a work the magnitude of which may be estimated, exacted, or paid for according to a definite standard, but free also in the sense that, while the mind, no doubt, occupies itself, still it does so

without ulterior regard to any other end, and yet with a feeling of satisfaction and stimulation (independent of reward).[16]

Whereas a unique content is required of prose, in poetry it is the unique form which is dominant and lasting. It is the sound, the rhythm, the physical relations among words . . . which predominates, at the expense of their capacity to be consumed as a definite, indisputable meaning.[17]

The economy of the work of art is thus organized around a signifying surplus that transcends the mere exchange between signifiers and signifieds, between tenors and vehicles. This excess, which engenders poetic value, constitutes, with respect to the system of exchange of equivalents, both its other and its *raison d'être*. For the exchange system—which has by no means disappeared, since it serves as a negative point of comparison for the production of poetic value—no longer exists in the service of the *comparable* (the "definite, indisputable meaning"), but, paradoxically, now functions in the service of the *incomparable,* the flower of poetry "Itself". "Poetry," writes Baudelaire, "cannot, under pain of death or decay, be assimilated with science or morality; it does not have truth as its object, it has only Itself."[18] This same idea perpetuates itself today in Jakobson's well-known definition of the poetic function: "The set (*Einstellung*) toward the MESSAGE as such, focus on the message for its own sake, is the POETIC function of language."[19]

How can we understand this paradoxical relation between a system of metaphorical equivalence and the engendering of its own transcendence? Curiously, Marx describes in these same terms the relation between a system of direct exchange and the emergence of capitalism. Let us compare a number of parallel extracts from poetic and economic texts:

Marx: A particular kind of commodity acquires the character of *universal equivalent,* because all other commodities make it the material in which they uniformly express their value.[20]

> *Baudelaire:* . . . tout vous ressemble, mon cher ange, . . . Ces trésors, ces meubles, ce luxe, cet ordre, ces parfums, ces fleurs miraculeuses, *c'est toi.*

Marx: The commodity that figures as universal equivalent is . . . *excluded* from the relative value form. (P. 68) This equivalent *has no relative form of value in common* with other commodities. (P. 69)

> *Baudelaire:* Fleur *incomparable . . .*

Marx: The simple circulation of commodities—selling in order to buy— is a means of carrying out a purpose unconnected with circulation, namely, the appropriation of use-values, the satisfaction of wants. The circulation of money as capital is, on the contrary, *an end in itself.* (P. 151)

> *Baudelaire:* La poésie . . . n'a pas la Vérité pour objet, elle n'a qu'*Elle-même.*

Marx: The circulation of capital has therefore no *limits.* (P. 152)

> *Baudelaire:* Ces énormes navires . . . tout chargés de *richesses* . . . ce sont mes pensées . . . . Tu les conduis doucement vers la mer qui est *l'Infini.*

Marx: The exact form of this process is therefore M-C-M$'$ [money-commodity-money+], where M$'$ = M+ Δ M = the original sum advanced, plus an increment. This increment or excess over the original value I call *"surplus-value."* The value originally advanced, therefore, not only remains intact while in circulation, but adds to itself a surplus-value or expands itself. It is this movement that converts it into capital. (P. 150, emphasis in original).

> *Baudelaire:* . . . là-bas, où les heures *plus* lentes contiennent *plus* de pensées, où les horloges sonnent le bonheur avec une *plus* profonde et *plus* significative solennité. . . . ce sont mes pensées *enrichies* qui reviennent.
>
> [There where the slower hours contain more thoughts, where the clocks toll

happiness with a more profound and
more significant solemnity.]

The message spelled out by this collage of quotations is certainly
not simple, but it incontestably suggests a resemblance between Poetry
and Capital, through their common way of transcending a system of
equivalences *in the very process of perpetuating it.* The circulation of
language as poetry is strikingly similar to the circulation of money as
capital, and the "poetic" could indeed be defined as *the surplus-value
of language.*

In combining metaphors of commerce with a panegyric to the priceless, the prose poem thus succeeds both in thematizing the traditional
opposition between the poetic and the economic and in subverting that
very opposition by inscribing a capitalistic model behind the structure
of poeticity. But if in the very act of proclaiming its opposition to and
transcendence of the economy of exchange—which is taken as "economy" per se—poetry parallels the logic of capital, then poetry's blindness
to its own resemblance with economic structures is hardly accidental.
On the contrary, it would seem that this type of misapprehension and
denial of its relation to other codes might be constitutive of poetry as
such. In fact, it seems that the function of the prose poem is precisely
to reveal what poetry is blind to about itself, not by in turn opposing
the poetic as such, but by making its functioning more explicit.

The Sweet Native Language

Telle est la puissance imaginaire des horticulteurs que, tout en regardant leur
spéculation comme manquée à l'avance, ils ne pensèrent plus . . . qu'à cette
grande tulipe noire réputée chimérique comme le cygne noir d'Horace et
comme le merle blanc de la tradition française.

—Alexandre Dumas père, *La Tulipe noire*

Vous n'êtes rien, frêles beautés,
Au *prix* des rêves enchantés
Qui tourbillonnent dans sa tête.
Nulle part il ne voit complète
        L'oeuvre de Dieu,
Il rêve le dahlia bleu.

—Pierre Dupont, *Le Dahlia bleu*

In the economy of the prose *Invitation,* the "you" with which all
is equated, the "flower" at once incomparable and infinitely comparable, thus serves as the universal equivalent, and hence represents poetry "Itself." It is doubtless not by chance that poetry should here be
represented by a flower: the poetic entity to which this prose poem

most directly refers is precisely a *Fleur du Mal.* Perhaps the true addressee of this poem is not a lady but a lyric: *L'Invitation au voyage* in
verse. It is thus between two *texts* that the true dialogue of the prose
poem situates itself.

But the textuality of this "allegorical flower" is not confined to
its reference to a *Fleur du Mal.* For far from consisting simply of new
or warmed-over Baudelairian rhetoric, this incomparable flower is also
designated by the names of two other well-known literary works—
Alexandre Dumas's *Black Tulip* and Pierre Dupont's *Blue Dahlia*—both
of which had become, in Baudelaire's day, common clichés for an un-
attainable ideal. We thus find ourselves confronted with a paradox: this
exceptional, incomparable flower ("qu'ils cherchent . . . j'ai trouvé"),
this uniquely personal possession (*"Moi,* j'ai trouvé *ma* tulipe noire et
mon dahlia bleu"), turns out to be, in truth, an impersonal linguistic
commonplace, a perfectly ordinary find. What could be the function
of this use of devalued language to express the highest poetic value?
What is the relation between the exceptional and the common, the
priceless and the devalued? In making of the incomparable a cliché, is
Baudelaire not reversing his own system of poetic values? The use of
these two commonplaces in a context that seems to call rather for
some strikingly novel expression indeed runs counter to the cult of
originality which has always underlain romantic poetry. Even as fine a
critic as Georges Blin finds himself disconcerted by this flagrant descent
to banality:

> There is an extraordinary gap between the banality of the contemporary
> references (to a popular novel and a poem) and, on the other hand, the lyri-
> cism, in blue and black, that for us, a century later, constitutes their mystery.
> What was the author's intention?[21]

But what the prose poem puts in question here is the very postulate of
the unity of the subject presupposed by this notion of "author's intention." Italicized in the text, the *black tulip* and the *blue dahlia* designate not the apotheosis of the quest, but the unsettling of the authority
of the quester. The typographical change is a change of voice, or rather
an ungovernable pluralization of the "sources" of language. What, indeed, is a cliché, but an authorless quotation? The question is thus not,
as Blin seems to phrase it, Who is speaking here, the *je* or the *on?* but
rather, Can the act of speaking have *one* subject? Can the boundary line
between *je* and *on* ever really be determined?

The "sweet native language" postulated by the verse poem is thus
no longer the unique, primal language of a unique individual, but rather
the authorless language of commonplaces and borrowed discourse,

through which man is born into language not as a speaking subject, but as a *spoken* subject.

In making explicit the process of stereotypization which underlies all language as both the result and the source of poetic discourse, Baudelaire's prose poem indeed predicts, in the same breath, its own valorization and its own devaluation:

> Un musicien a écrit l'*Invitation à la valse;* quel est celui qui composera l'*Invitation au voyage,* qu'on puisse offrir à la femme aimée, à la soeur d'élection? (Emphasis in original)

> [A musician has written the *Invitation to the Waltz;* who will be the one to compose an *Invitation to the Voyage* that one can offer to the beloved woman, to the chosen sister?]

In citing its own title as a future offering to the beloved, the text here already refers to itself as a potential cliché, as a currency of seduction coined to participate in a stereotyped ritual of exchange. Through its own self-quotation, the *Invitation au voyage* reads itself, like the land of Cockaigne and the black tulip, as the linguistic property of *on*, not yet written but already part of historical repetition.

From the commonplace flower (black tulip, blue dahlia) to the commonplace land (the land of Cockaigne), from the "you" of the home port to the "you" of the exotic shore, the entire poetic voyage thus takes place within the familiar bounds of clichés: rhetorical displacement in effect never leaves the common place. This familiar commonplace (indeed, universally equivalent with *all*) is, however, at the same time strangely foreign; its appeal is that of an unfamiliar, "unknown land." But the *"nostalgia* for an *unknown* land" ("cette *nostalgie* du pays qu'on *ignore"*) which motivates the voyage is not, paradoxically, an attraction to the absolutely new, but the fascination of an invitation to *return,* of a call to "come back":

> . . . de toutes choses, de tous les coins, des fissures des tiroirs et des plis des étoffes s'échappe un parfum singulier, un *revenez-y* de Sumatra, qui est comme l'âme de l'appartement.
>
> Un vrai pays de Cocagne, te dis-je . . . (Emphasis in original)

> [. . . from all things, from all corners, from the cracks in the drawers and from the folds in the fabrics springs a singular perfume, a *come back* from Sumatra, which is like the soul of the apartment.
>
> A veritable land of Cockaigne, I tell you . . .]

The invitation to return, whose source, as Baudelaire's italics indicate (*"revenez-y"*), is in another text—an Other text—marks the call of the familiar as unfamiliar. The voyage to the land "which one could call the Orient of the Occident" ("qu'on pourrait appeler l'Orient de l'Occident") here becomes not the search for some faraway utopia, but the quest for what (dis)orients all return and all repetition, a quest, in other words, for what subverts the very *sense*—or direction—of the voyage. If u-topia (no-place) and the common-place are ultimately indistinguishable (as Dumas indeed suggests by comparing his utopian black tulip to the "white crow of the French tradition" and to the "black swan of Horace"), it can only be because the truly unreachable utopian place, the place which is par excellence unknowable, is not some faraway mysterious land, but the very place where *one is*.

Correction and Extension

> Ce qui était poème redevient prose, et les éléments inédits qui auraient dû renouveler le sujet, paraissent surajoutés intellectuellement.
>
> —Henri Brugmans, *"L'Invitation au voyage* de Baudelaire"

In contrast to the lyrical *Invitation,* which seeks to return to a "native" language and a state of primal, natural integrity anterior to social, temporal, and rhetorical differentiation, the prose poem, which reevaluates the devalued language of clichés, explicitly privileges artistic belatedness over natural firstness:

> Pays singular, supérieur aux autres, *comme l'Art l'est à la Nature,* où celle-ci est *réformée* par le rêve, où elle est *corrigée, embellie, refondue.*
>
> [A singular land, superior to the others, *as Art is superior to Nature,* where Nature is *revised* by dream, where it is *corrected, embellished, reworked.*]

It is tempting to consider this valorization of correction and revision as a description of the prose poem's own status with respect to the verse poem, which can easily be seen as the "Nature" that must be reformed, the "raw material" or pre-text to which the prose poem's "Art" is applied. Indeed, the importance of the process of revision and transformation is constantly thematized in the prose poem through the ubiquitous use of verbs of transformation: *illustrer, bâtir, décorer, allonger, colorer, tamiser, ouvrager, diviser, réformer, corriger, embellir, refondre, chercher, reculer, éloigner, peindre,* and even *cuisiner.*

But how does the work of transformation manifest itself concretely in the textual relations between the two *Invitations?*

Compared with the spare verticality of the verse poem, the well-filled paragraphs of the prose poem have always led readers to consider the prose as an expanded version of the "same poetic idea,"[22] translated into a freer, more verbose style. According to J. B. Ratermanis, the prose poem is constructed "by the successive development of elements whose main points (and not more than that!) are provided by the verse poem; some of the associations they contain are simply made more explicit."[23] For Suzanne Bernard, "all of what was merely suggested or implicit in the verse poem is now taken up again, detailed and circumstantiated in the prose."[24] Whether these additions are then considered appropriate or foreign to the original idea, whether their presence is "jarring"[25] or raises the text's "seduction" to its "peak,"[26] the governing principle behind the prose poem's elaboration remains the same: it consists of repeating, developing, expanding, and making explicit the contents of the verse poem.

This conception of the prose poem as the amplification of a repeated poetic kernel seems to be confirmed by the structure of the prose *Invitation*; through the repeated return of certain opening lines ("Il est un pays . . . un pays de Cocagne . . . un vrai pays de Cocagne. . . . C'est là qu'il faut . . . Oui, c'est là qu'il faut . . ."etc.), the text takes shape by repeating and expanding upon its own starting points. Whereas verse is constructed out of the repetition of ends (rhymes), prose here develops by repeating its beginnings. The absence of any a priori limits to the extensibility of prose means that its measure can be taken only after the fact; in order to have reached an end, prose is only capable of marking a new beginning. It is perhaps this rhythm of returns and prolongations that conveys the impression that the prose poem is an amplified repetition of the verse poem, its "starting point." This impression is also supported by Baudelaire's description of his *Petits poèmes en prose* as still being "*Fleurs du Mal,* but with *much more* freedom, more detail, and more raillery."[27]

The common formula for the prose poem thus seems to read as follows: "It is still the same thing (as the verse), but with much more: prose = verse + *X*." However, should this formula be taken literally? Is the process of correction really mere addition, simple explicitation, pure secondary elaboration of the "same poetic idea"? What, in other words, is the status of what the prose poem is supposed to be repeating?

In order to investigate this question, let us compare the verse and prose versions of the "refrain":

Là, tout n'est qu'ordre et beauté,
Luxe, calme et volupté

Un vrai pays de Cocagne, où tout est
beau, riche, tranquille, honnête; où
le luxe a plaisir à se mirer dans
l'ordre; où la vie est grasse et
douce à respirer; d'où le désordre,
la turbulence et l'imprévu sont exclus;

où le bonheur est marié au silence;
où la cuisine elle-même est poétique,
grasse et excitante à la fois, où
tout vous ressemble, mon cher ange.

[There, all is but order and beauty,/   [A veritable land of Cockaigne, where
Luxury, calm, and sensual pleasure.]   all is beautiful, rich, tranquil, honest;
                                              where luxury is pleased to mirror itself
                                              in order; where life is rich and sweet to
                                              breathe; where disorder, turmoil, and
                                              the unforeseen are excluded; where
                                              happiness is married to silence; where
                                              the cooking itself is poetic, rich and
                                              stimulating at once, where all resembles
                                              you, my dear angel.]

We have already pointed out the dissonant effect produced by the sudden appearance of the word *honest* in the prose version. However, this inclusion of a bourgeois value in a poetic context is not a simple addition of a new value to the existing ones, but rather, a transformation of the very notion of value. The very dissonance between the positive values of esthetics and those of ethics makes explicit the negativity—the purely differential nature—of linguistic values. For while *tranquil* alone is more or less synonymous with the verse refrain's *calm*, this correspondence is suddenly broken by the contamination of the word *honest*. *Tranquillity* becomes retrospectively different from itself, evoking not the quiet harmony of an exotic landscape, but the safety of a proprietor secure in the civil order that guarantees both his freedom and his property. In the same way, while *order* and *luxury* had in the verse poem been separated by *beauty*, which gave them an esthetic coloring, their relation in the prose poem no longer has anything esthetic about it: luxury mirrors itself in the *law-and-order*[28] of institutionalized forces designed to protect and perpetuate it. And the word *sweet*, which in the verse poem conveyed a delicate tenderness ("Songe à   la *douceur*"), here becomes a mere condiment, making life into a tasty consumer product ("la vie est grasse et *douce* à respirer"). What is added to the lyric vocabulary is not simply foreign to it; in the transformation produced by these additions, it is the repeated elements which become somehow foreign to themselves. In this struggle between codes, it thus becomes impossible to determine where one code ends and another begins. And if, as the critics would have it, the prose poem repeats the "same theme" as the verse poem, it is in order to question both the idea of *same* and the idea of *theme*.

This differential work of supplementation, in which the "same" becomes the "other," is explicitly described in the poem:

Pays singulier, noyé dans les brumes de notre Nord, et qu'on pourrait appeler l'Orient de l'Occident, la Chine de l'Europe, tant la chaude et capricieuse fantaisie s'y est donné carrière, tant elle l'a patiemment et opiniâtrement illustré de ses savantes et délicates végétations.

[A singular land, drowned in the mists of our North, and which could be called the Orient of the Occident, the China of Europe, so freely has warm, capricious fantasy acted on it, patiently and stubbornly illustrating it with knowing and delicate vegetations.]

This rhetorical transformation of the Occident into the Orient by the illustration of fantasy can easily be seen as the very image of the prose poem's "explicitation" of its versified original. Indeed, is not this singular land, which could be called "the Other of the Same," precisely what poetry has become? For it is not prose that is here opposed to poetry, but poetry that, reworked by prose, has separated from itself—not by becoming what it is not, but by making manifest its status as a pure linguistic value, constituted by its own difference from itself.

Correction and Castration

Nous pouvons couper où nous voulons . . .
    —Baudelaire, *Dédicace aux Petits poèmes en prose*

Our examination of the validity of the formula ("prose = verse + *X*") that underlies the traditional analysis of this text has brought us to the point at which it is no longer possible to distinguish the "same" ("verse") from the "other"("*X*"). But even the most literal-minded attempt to divide the text of the prose poem into what is repeated and what is added soon reveals not only that this distinction is inoperative, but that the text of the verse poem has to a large extent materially disappeared. Let us compare, for example, the following extracts:

D'aller là-bas vivre ensemble!
  Aimer à loisir
  Aimer et mourir
	C'est là qu'il faut aller vivre, c'est là
	qu'il faut aller mourir.

[To go there to live together!/To love at leisure,/To love and die]	[It is there that one must go to live, it is there that one must go to die.]

In the verse poem, the words *live* and *die* are mediated by the repetition of the word *love,* which gives them an erotic connotation. But in the prose, *live* and *die* are juxtaposed without any *love:* the voyage could just as well be solitary as amorous. This elimination of the word *love* from what is supposed to be a love poem may seem surprising. But if we add up everything the prose poem does *not* repeat, we find that "charmes," "tes yeux," "larmes," "beauté," "volupté," "chambre," "assouvir," and "désir" have been eliminated along with "aimer" and "ensemble." What has disappeared in the passage from verse to prose is the very process of seduction.

The text of the verse poem has thus not simply been mounted in prose like a jewel in a new setting. Before being "repeated," the verse poem has had its main erotic moments amputated. This process of amputation is at work on a formal level as well: the transformation of verse into prose involves a similar elimination of the moments of intensity (rhythm, rhyme) which give poetry its seductive charm. It is not by chance that what the prose poem cuts out of the lyric is its eroticism. For this textual amputation, this suppression of the lyric's semantic and formal potency, corresponds quite literally to the moment of castration.

That castration is somehow constitutive of the prose poem is repeatedly suggested throughout the various texts of Baudelaire's *Petits poèmes en prose,* where metaphors of violent blows and cuts indeed proliferate.[29] In *Perte d'Auréole (Loss of Halo),* in which Baudelaire specifically allegorizes the passage from poetry to prose, the amputation of the poet's halo—the "insignia" of his poetic power—necessarily precedes his entry into the "mauvais lieu" of mere prose. And the breaking up of versification itself is perhaps dramatized in the *Mauvais Vitrier:* the poet's gesture of smashing the panes of glass can be read as a play on the pun "briser les verres" ("smashing glass") = "briser les vers" ("smashing verse"). The passage from poetry to prose seems to involve an amputation of everything which, in poetry, is erected as unity, totality, immortality, and potency.

Exclusion/Inclusion: Poetry and Its Double

> Aimer une femme, passe encore, mais une statue, quelle sottise!
>
> —Flaubert, *La Tentation de Saint-Antoine*

But what is the true nature of this potent poetic unity and totality, which is denatured and mutilated by the prose? What does the integrity of the lyric code—the "before" of the moment of castration—in fact comprise? The lyric seems to answer:

> Là, tout n'est qu'ordre et beauté,
> Luxe, calme et volupté.

It is this harmonious "all," this image of indivisible totality, which becomes, in the prose,

> Un vrai pays de Cocagne, où tout est beau, riche, tranquille, honnête; où le
> luxe a plaisir à se mirer dans l'ordre; où la vie est grasse et douce à respirer;
> d'où le désordre, la turbulence et l'imprévu sont exclus; où le bonheur est
> marié au silence . . .

"All is but order and beauty;" "Where all is beautiful, rich, tranquil, honest": the evocation, in both cases, begins with the word *all*. And since it is precisely the notion of totality which is in question, since it is toward totality that poetry aspires—the subject's unity or the incestuous union in the perfect metaphorical return to the origin—an analysis of the function of the word *all* in the two texts may indeed turn out to be revealing.

We have already noted that, in the verse poem, this totality results not from infinite inclusiveness but rather from restrictive exclusiveness ("Tout *n'est que* . . ."). The list of abstractions which compose this totality ("ordre," "beauté," "luxe," "calme," "volupté") are superimposed upon each other like metaphorical mirrors of one unique poetic essence ("tout"). In the prose poem, on the other hand, the verb *être* is no longer limited a priori by a restrictive construction ("ne . . . que"), and, in the place of the paradigmatic series of equivalent abstractions, we find a syntagmatic list of descriptive adjectives and arbitrarily juxtaposed details subordinated to the adverb "où" ("where"). Thus consisting of an extensible collection of miscellaneous properties and fragmentary descriptions, the prosaic *all* is metonymic rather than metaphoric, inclusive rather than exclusive, circumstantial rather than essential. The passage from essence to attribute is a passage from totality to partition; while the poetic *all* is as such indivisible, the prose poem's *all* is divided into a series of attributes whose number can be indefinitely increased without being able to exhaust the meaning of *all,* the sum of which the enumeration indefinitely defers. In becoming, through its infinite extensibility, the conflictual locus of a struggle among heterogeneous and incompatible codes, the "tout est" of the prose does not thereby designate, however, another specific code that would as such be opposed to the poetic one ("realism," "prose," "ordinary language"); rather, the prose "tout est" allegorically represents the code of the non-totality of all codes. "All is," in other words, names not a totality but a *set,* a set of codes, that is, a set of sets. And just as modern set theory entails the fundamental paradox that "the set of all the sets in a universe is not a set," the "tout est" of the prose poem demonstrates that the code of all the codes in a semiological universe cannot, in turn, become a code.

Among the diverse attributes of the land of Cockaigne, the following is particularly significant: "le désordre, la turbulence et l'imprévu *sont exclus"* ("disorder, turmoil, and the unforeseen *are excluded"*). Could this exclusion of disorder not be read as an explicitation of the implicit exclusivity in the verse poem's "tout n'est qu'ordre"? If so, then the prosaic transformation of the poetic abstractions ("order," "beauty," "luxury," "calm," "pleasure") into a series of descriptive properties—properties that introduce into the prose poem economic and social codes foreign to the poetic code—is not simply a secondary elaboration: it is an explicitation of what the abstractions were original-ly abstracted from, of that from which the verse poem's refrain re-frained. The poetic code is thus not simply a set of elements considered "poetic" but also a process of exclusion and of negation, of active re-pression of whatever belongs to other codes. If, then, as Georges Blin puts it, Baudelaire's prose poems literally contain *"what is excluded* from *Les Fleurs du Mal,"*[30] their function is to make explicit not only *what* poetry excludes, but its very constitutive *act of excluding*.

That the act of excluding and cutting might in fact be constitutive of poetry as such is suggested not only by the "ne . . . que" syntax of the lyric *Invitation* but also by the insistence of exclusive formulations in Baudelaire's general remarks about poetry:

> La Poésie . . . *n'a pas* d'autre but *qu'*Elle-même . . . elle *n'a pas* la Vérité pour objet, elle *n'a qu'*Elle-même.

> [Poetry . . . has *no* end *other than* Itself . . . it does *not* have Truth as its ob-ject, it has *only* Itself.]

In viewing itself as the unmediated voice of the soul, as the original expression of subjectivity, poetry is blind both to its own status as a code, and to its relation to other codes, that is, to its own necessary mutilation produced by the very process of exclusion on which its sense of wholeness and uniqueness in fact depends. The forces of order which guard the poetic frontier are designed not only to repress, but to erase—wipe clean—the very traces of repression, the very traces of the cleaning operation. Only then can poetry—"propre et luisante comme une belle conscience"—seem to be "pure," that is, cut off from the process of its own production, from any history or context that is not Itself; cut off by what Jacques Derrida has called "a pure cut without negativity, a *without* without negativity and without meaning."[31]

This obliteration and forgetting of the process of production and the consequent overestimation of the object produced, this erection of a fixed, statufied form as proof against mutilation and incompleteness, is characteristic of what both Marx and Freud have called fetishism. Both as a monument set up against the horror of castration and as a seem-ingly "mystical"[32] product divorced from the work of its production, poetry—the potency and seemingly inexhaustible wealth of language—indeed reifies itself into a sort of linguistic fetish. Fixed in its "pure," immortal form, erected against the "movement that displaces lines" ("le mouvement qui déplace les lignes"),[33] poetry, like Beauty in Baudelaire's well-known sonnet of that name, is nothing other than a "dream of stone" ("rêve de pierre"), the very image of death, castration, and repression which it is designed to block out and to occult.

If the prose poem thus consists of a textual act of subversion of the fetish, of the amputation of the lyric text, the verse poem in its turn, through its fundamental gesture of exclusion ("tout *n'est que* . . ."), was already constituted by a process of mutilation and occultation of another text, a heterogeneous cultural text strained by conflicts among codes—a text, indeed, that very much resembles the *Invitation au voyage* in prose.

Between the prose poem and the verse poem, in other words, the work of mutilation and correction operates indefinitely *in both directions*. Each of the two texts is the pre-text of the other; neither can claim priority over the other: the "raw material" is always already a mutilated text. This reciprocal correction is, however, not symmetrical: while it is the diverse heterogeneity of cultural codes which is excluded from the verse, the infinite inclusiveness of the prose extends as far as to include the very gesture of exclusion. But to include the exclusion of inclusiveness is to erase or put in question the very boundary between the inside and the outside, the very limits of poetic space. In doing so, the prose poem ultimately questions its own exteriority to poetry ("prose") as well as its interiority to it ("poem"). Internally external to the poetry it both repeats and estranges from itself, the prose poem becomes the place where castration and fetishization, valorization and devaluation, repression and subversion, simultaneously oppose each other and undermine their very opposition. Neither poetry's "other" nor its "same," the prose poem thus constitutes nothing less than poetry's *double:* its double space as the space of its own division, as its "other stage" where what has been repressed by poetry interminably returns in the uncanny figures of its strange familiarity, where poetry, the linguistic fetish, the "dream of stone"—whether a *Commendatore*'s statue or an implacable Venus with marble eyes[34] —suddenly begins to speak from out of the Other, from out of what is constituted by its very inability to determine its own limits.

Appendix

L'Invitation au voyage (Verse)

> Mon enfant, ma soeur,
> Songe à la douceur
> D'aller là-bas vivre ensemble!
> Aimer à loisir,
> Aimer et mourir
> Au pays qui te ressemble!
> Les soleils mouillés
> De ces ciels brouillés
> Pour mon esprit ont les charmes
> Si mystérieux
> De tes traîtres yeux,
> Brillant à travers leurs larmes.
>
> Là, tout n'est qu'ordre et beauté,
> Luxe, calme et volupté.
>
> Des meubles luisants,
> Polis par les ans,
> Décoreraient notre chambre;
> Les plus rares fleurs
> Mêlant leurs odeurs
> Aux vagues senteurs de l'ambre,
> Les riches plafonds,
> Les miroirs profonds,
> La splendeur orientale,
> Tout y parlerait
> A l'âme en secret
> Sa douce langue natale.
>
> Là, tout n'est qu'ordre et beauté,
> Luxe, calme et volupté.
>
> Vois sur ces canaux
> Dormir ces vaisseaux
> Dont l'humeur est vagabonde;
> C'est pour assouvir
> Ton moindre désir
> Qu'ils viennent du bout du monde.
> —Les soleils couchants
> Revêtent les champs,
> Les canaux, la ville entière,

D'hyacinthe et d'or;
Le monde s'endort
Dans une chaude lumière.

Là, tout n'est qu'ordre et beauté,
Luxe, calme et volupté.

L'Invitation au voyage (Prose)

Il est un pays superbe, un pays de Cocagne, dit-on, que je rêve de visiter avec une vieille amie. Pays singulier, noyé dans les brumes de notre Nord, et qu'on pourrait appeler l'Orient de l'Occident, la Chine de l'Europe, tant la chaude et capricieuse fantaisie s'y est donné carrière, tant elle l'a patiemment et opiniâtrement illustré de ses savantes et délicates végétations.

Un vrai pays de Cocagne, où tout est beau, riche, tranquille, honnête; où le luxe a plaisir à se mirer dans l'ordre; où la vie est grasse et douce à respirer; d'où le désordre, la turbulence et l'imprévu sont exclus; où le bonheur est marié au silence; où la cuisine elle-même est poétique, grasse et excitante à la fois; où tout vous ressemble, mon cher ange.

Tu connais cette maladie fiévreuse qui s'empare de nous dans les froides misères, cette nostalgie du pays qu'on ignore, cette angoisse de la curiosité? Il est une contrée qui te ressemble, où tout est beau, riche, tranquille et honnête, où la fantaisie a bâti et décoré une Chine occidentale, où la vie est douce à respirer, où le bonheur est marié au silence. C'est là qu'il faut aller vivre, c'est là qu'il faut aller mourir!

Oui, c'est là qu'il faut aller respirer, rêver et allonger les heures par l'infini des sensations. Un musicien a écrit l'*Invitation à la valse;* quel est celui qui composera l'*Invitation au voyage,* qu'on puisse offrir à la femme aimée, à la soeur d'élection?

Oui, c'est dans cette atmosphère qu'il ferait bon vivre,—là-bas, où les heures plus lentes contiennent plus de pensées, où les horloges sonnent le bonheur avec une plus profonde et plus significative solennité.

Sur des panneaux luisants, ou sur des cuirs dorés et d'une richesse sombre, vivent discrètement des peintures béates, calmes et profondes, comme les âmes des artistes qui les créèrent. Les soleils couchants, qui colorent si richement la salle à manger ou le salon, sont tamisés par de belles étoffes ou par ces hautes fenêtres ouvragées que le plomb divise en nombreux compartiments. Les meubles sont vastes, curieux, bizarres, armés de serrures et de secrets comme des âmes raffinées. Les miroirs, les métaux, les étoffes, l'orfévrerie et la faience y jouent pour les yeux une symphonie muette et mystérieuse; et de toutes choses, de tous les coins, des fissures des tiroirs et des plis des étoffes s'échappe un parfum singulier, un *revenez-y* de Sumatra, qui est comme l'âme de l'appartement.

Un vrai pays de Cocagne, te dis-je, où tout est riche, propre et luisant, comme une belle conscience, comme une magnifique batterie de cuisine, comme une splendide orfévrerie, comme une bijouterie bariolée! Les trésors du monde y affluent, comme dans la maison d'un homme laborieux et qui a bien mérité du monde entier. Pays singulier, supérieur aux autres, comme l'Art l'est à la Nature, où celle-ci est ré-formée par le rêve, où elle est corrigée, embellie, refondue.

Qu'ils cherchent, qu'ils cherchent encore, qu'ils reculent sans cesse les limites de leur bonheur, ces alchimistes de l'horticulture! Qu'ils proposent des prix de soixante et de cent mille florins pour qui résoudra leurs ambitieux problèmes! Moi, j'ai trouvé ma *tulipe noire* et mon *dahlia bleu!*

Fleur incomparable, tulipe retrouvée, allégorique dahlia, c'est là, n'est-ce pas, dans ce beau pays si calme et si rêveur, qu'il faudrait aller vivre et fleurir? Ne serais-tu pas encadrée dans ton analogie, et ne pourrais-tu pas te mirer, pour parler comme les mystiques, dans ta propre *correspondance?*

Des rêves! toujours des rêves! et plus l'âme est ambitieuse et déli-cate, plus les rêves l'éloignent du possible. Chaque homme porte en lui sa dose d'opium naturel, incessament sécrétée et renouvelée, et, de la naissance à la mort, combien comptons-nous d'heures remplies par la jouissance positive, par l'action réussie et décidée? Vivrons-nous jamais, passerons-nous jamais dans ce tableau qu'a peint mon esprit, ce tableau qui te ressemble?

Ces trésors, ces meubles, ce luxe, cet ordre, ces parfums, ces fleurs miraculeuses, c'est toi. C'est encore toi, ces grands fleuves et ces canaux tranquilles. Ces énormes navires qu'ils charrient, tout chargés de rich-esses, et d'où montent les chants monotones de la manoeuvre, ce sont mes pensées qui dorment ou qui roulent sur ton sein. Tu les conduis doucement vers la mer qui est l'Infini, tout en réfléchissant les pro-fondeurs du ciel dans la limpidité de ta belle âme;—et quand, fatigués par la houle et gorgés des produits de l'Orient, ils rentrent au port natal, ce sont encore mes pensées enrichies qui reviennent de l'infini vers toi.

4. Poetry and Performative Language: Mallarmé and Austin

> Surely the words must be spoken "seriously" and so as to be taken "serious-ly"? This is, though vague, true enough in general—it is an important common-place in discussing the purport of any utterance whatsoever, I must not be joking, for example, nor writing a poem.
>
> —J. L. Austin, *How to Do Things with Words*

The Cry of the Occasion

> The poem is the cry of its occasion,
> Part of the res itself and not about it.
> —Wallace Stevens, "An Ordinary Evening in New Haven"

While rocking lazily in their landau through the late afternoon sun, an elegant lady and her escort happen upon a somewhat dilapidated but mysteriously crowded fairground. There, in an empty stand, the lady remedies the absence of any proper performer by waking up the drum-mer, setting her escort up as a fee-collecting barker, and mounting a table to enigmatically exhibit herself to the crowd. The gentleman, in-stantly comprehending his duty in this tricky situation, glances at the lady's hair and recites a sonnet, after which, lifting her down from the table, he adds a more plain-folks explanation of the spectacle. The two then make their way, amid the puzzled approbation of the onlookers, back toward their carriage through the now-dark open air, cozily dis-cussing the performance they have just given.

So runs, more or less, the "plot" of Mallarmé's prose poem *La Déclaration foraine*. The questions raised by this text are legion. What (if anything) is being declared (about poetry?) and how does it relate to other moments in Mallarmé's writings? What is the relation between the sonnet and the lady on the one hand, and between the verse and the

52

prose on the other? How does the narrative frame motivate the existence of the verse poem? In other words, *when,* according to this text, does it make sense that there be a poem?

On its most obvious level, *La Déclaration foraine* is the story of an improvised side show composed of two parts: a motionless woman and a spoken poem. In the context, the relation between the two seems deceptively transparent: the sonnet ("*La chevelure vol d'une flamme . . .*") is simply, as Robert Greer Cohn describes it, "a celebration of a woman whose looks, featuring magnificent hair, need no outer adornment."[1] The poet's act would thus seem to bear out Remy de Gourmont's affirmation that "all things in life having been said thousands and thousands of times, the poet can no longer do anything but point to them, accompanying his gesture with a few murmured words."[2] In its simultaneous act of naming and exhibiting, the poem can thus be said to relate to the lady as a sign to its referent.

But if that is the case, how does this poem fit in with the rest of Mallarmé's poetics of "suggestion," which he explicitly opposes to literal denomination?[3] If one recalls Mallarmé's repeated insistence on poetry's abolition of simple referentiality, on the "vibratory near-disappearance" of the real object "on which the pages would have trouble closing," one begins to suspect two things: that the traditional reading of Mallarmé's nonreferentiality is inadequate and that the lady's hair is only the apparent subject of the sonnet, the "indifferent" or "surface" meaning that both hides and reveals something to which it remains "exterior."[4] Mallarmé's own highly ambiguous statement of the noncorrespondence between the obvious and the true in his own work is probably responsible for the universal critical tendency to give the hair a symbolic meaning, to find the "pure notion" or "idea"—Poetry, ideal Beauty, naked Truth, Promethean fire, provocative Femininity—behind the materiality of the *chevelure*. The prose poem, in fact, expressly invites a reading of this type by calling the lady a "living allegory," which further problematizes, but does not eliminate, the question of the poem's referentiality.

But whatever may be said about the lady's flaming mane, it is not the hair or any of its symbolic substitutes that is being discussed in the concluding dialogue of the piece, but rather the conditions of possibility of the emission and reception of the sonnet itself. Poetry, if it is indeed the "subject" of the poem, becomes here not some ideal and statuesque concept, but a function of a specific interlocutionary situation, an *act of speech,* the lady banteringly tells her escort, that

> vous n'auriez peut-être pas introduit, qui sait? mon ami, le prétexte de formuler ainsi devant moi au conjoint isolement par exemple de notre voiture—où

est-elle—regagnons-la;—mais ceci jaillit, forcé, sous le coup de poing brutal à
l'estomac, que cause une impatience de gens auxquels coûte que coûte et
soudain il faut proclamer quelque chose fût-ce la rêverie . . .

—Qui s'ignore et se lance nue de peur, en travers du public; c'est vrai.
Comme vous, Madame, ne l'auriez entendu si irréfutablement, malgré sa ré-
duplication sur une rime du trait final, mon boniment d'après un mode primitif
du sonnet, je le gage, si chaque terme ne s'en était répercuté jusqu'à vous par
de variés tympans, pour charmer un esprit ouvert à la compréhension multiple.

—Peut-être! accepta notre pensée dans un enjouement de souffle nocturne
la même.

[you would perhaps not have introduced, who knows? my friend, the pretext
of formulating thus before me in the joint isolation for example of our carriage
—where is it—let's return to it;—but this spews forth, by force, from the brutal
punch in the stomach caused by an impatience of people to whom at all costs
and suddenly something must be proclaimed even a reverie . . .

—Which does not know itself and hurls itself naked with fear through the
audience; that's true. Just as you, Madame, would not have heard and understood it so irrefutably, in spite of its reduplication on a rhyme in the final
thrust, my spiel composed after a primitive mode of the sonnet, I bet, if each
term of it had not bounced back to you off a variety of eardrums, to charm a
mind open to multiple comprehension.

—Perhaps! accepted our thought in a cheekiness of night air the same.]

The story of the recitation of an occasional poem thus concludes
with a discussion of what constitutes a poem's occasion; the two ex-
performers are interested not in what the poem means, but in how it
means, and in how it managed to come into being at all. Two conditions, whose significance we will discuss later, appear necessary for the
poem to occur: audience and violence. Without them, the poet would
"perhaps," "who knows?" not have introduced the "pretext of formulating" his poem into the silent, isolated togetherness of the rocking
coach. In fact, the prose poem, which ends by discussing the necessary
conditions for the production of speech, begins by triply insisting on a
state of *absence* of speech:

Le *Silence!* il est certain qu'à mon côté, ainsi que songes, étendue dans un
bercement de promenade sous les roues assoupissant l'interjection de fleurs,
toute femme, et j'en sais une qui voit clair ici, *m'exempte de l'effort à proférer
un vocable:* la *complimenter haut* de quelque interrogatrice toilette, offre de
soi presque à l'homme en faveur de qui s'achève l'après-midi, *ne pouvant* à
l'encontre de tout ce rapprochement fortuit, *que suggérer la distance* sur ses
traits aboutie à une fossette de spirituel sourire. (Emphasis mine here and
passim)

[Silence! it is certain that at my side, as maybe dream, lying back in a
rocking drive while the wheels are assuaging the interjection of flowers, any
woman, and I know one who sees through this, exempts me from the effort of
proffering a single vocable: to compliment her aloud on some interrogative

toilette, offer of self almost to the man in favor of whom the afternoon draws
to a close, serving with respect to all this fortuitous closeness only to suggest
distance on her features ending in a dimple of bantering smile.]

The simple juxtaposition between the "declaration" in the title and the
"Silence" in the opening line should thus, from the beginning, warn us
that "to speak or not to speak" is, in some way, the question. Moreover, a glance at the vocabulary of the text reveals an overwhelming
number of references to speech acts: verbs (*exempter, proférer, complimenter, suggérer, consentir, nommer, témoigner, proposer, conjurer,
dégoiser, dire, soupirer, diffamer, observer, ajouter, communiquer,
introduire, formuler, proclamer, gager, accepter*), nouns (*déclaration,
interjection, vocifération, explication, convocation, exhibition, pré-
somption, affectation, approbation*), and even adjectives (*interrogatrice,
appréciative*). This list resembles nothing so much as the concluding
chapter of J. L. Austin's *How to Do Things with Words,* in which an
attempt is made to draw up a list of what Austin calls "performative
utterances."

In order to determine whether the notion of the performative can
shed any light on our poem (and vice versa), let us now turn briefly to
Austin's description of its principal characteristics. First, a sentence is
called performative if it can be shown that "to utter the sentence . . . is
not to *describe* my doing of what I should be said in so uttering to be
doing or to state that I am doing it: it is to do it . . . . The name [per-
formative] is derived, of course, from 'perform,' the usual verb with the
noun 'action': it indicates that the issuing of the utterance is the per-
forming of an action"[5] (emphasis in original). Thus, for example, the
sentence "I declare war" is itself the act of declaring war, whereas "I
kill the enemy" is only a report of the act of killing the enemy. In
addition, according to Austin, the action performed by the utterance
must in some way belong to "an accepted conventional procedure
having a certain conventional effect."[6] And finally, "it is always
necessary that the *circumstances* in which the words are uttered should
be in some way, or ways, *appropriate.*"[7] One finds the performative,
then, whenever, in a given situation, *saying* something is *doing* something recognizable.

Without further qualification of these criteria, it could be said that
the very recitation of the sonnet in *La Déclaration foraine* could be
classed as a performative utterance: to utter the poem is visibly to perform the action of uttering a poem which, unorthodox as it may be, is
uncontestably made to fit into its side show circumstances. As for the
act's conventionality, the poet himself calls it a "lieu commun d'une

esthétique." Obviously, some further qualification of the specificity of a performative utterance is needed to distinguish it from the mere act of speaking, for, as Austin himself inquires, "When we issue any utterance whatsoever, are we not 'doing something'?"[8] In his attempts to find a formula inclusive of all speech acts in which saying is doing, Austin passes from consideration of grammatical form and transformational rules to considerations of semantic content and interpersonal effects. In the course of the inquiry, the original binary opposition between performative and constative language inevitably breaks down. The impossibility of defining the linguistic specificity of the performative utterance (for which we will try to account later on) leads Austin to draw up a new set of analytic terms focusing not on the intrinsic characteristics of an utterance but on its actual function in an interlocutionary situation. Abandoning the performative/constative dichotomy, Austin proposes to analyze any utterance according to three "dimensions": (1) the *locutionary* (sound, sense and reference), (2) the *illocutionary* (intentional and conventional force), and (3) the *perlocutionary* (actual effect).

Since these notions, though not without their usefulness, are at least as problematic as the notion of the performative, subsequent thinkers have preferred to return to the search for a set of stable linguistic criteria for the isolation of the performative. By choosing these criteria in such a way as to eliminate all but what Austin himself calls "*explicit* performatives" (emphasis in this paragraph in original), this task becomes relatively simple: explicit performatives are verbs in the first (or impersonal third) person singular present indicative active which possess "an *asymmetry* of a systematic kind [with respect to] other persons and tenses of the *very same word.*"[9] That is, to use Austin's example, "I bet" is the actual performance of the act of betting, whereas "he bets" is only a report of an act of betting. The performative is only operative if the action performed is "at the moment of uttering being done by the person uttering."[10] The performative, then, acts like a "shifter" in that it takes on meaning only by referring to the instance of its utterance. The French linguist Emile Benveniste, adding a self-referential semantic dimension to the definition, effectively eliminates any remaining uncertainty when he asserts that "an utterance is performative insofar as it *names* the act performed . . . . The utterance *is* the act; the utterer performs the act by naming it."[11]

This elimination of uncertainty is also, of course, an elimination of the unstated philosophical question behind the whole inquiry, of which the least that can be said is that it has something to do with the role of language in human power relationships. That is, Austin's original question was undoubtedly not, When do we know for sure that an utterance is performative? but, What kinds of things are we really *doing* when we speak? But before discussing the way in which our poem relates to this immense question, let us first examine the role of its "explicit," self-referential performative expressions.

Considered in the most restricted terms of the definition, only one of our numerous performative verbs can actually be classed as a "live" performance. This verb, as it happens, is precisely the verb *I bet* ("je le gage"), with which the poet closes his argument. Is it by chance that Mallarmé should choose this particular verb as the only operative performative in this text? In view of the relation between a bet and, say, a throw of dice, one suspects that it is not. But before pursuing this train of thought further, let us examine the function of the nonoperative performative expressions on our list.

Of these, most are temporally deactivated by being reported in the infinitive ("proférer," "complimenter," "suggérer") or in the third person ("toute femme . . . m'exempte") or in the past tense ("proposa," "consentit," "accepta"). That is, the speech act to which they refer is not being performed but only named or reported. The name of the deactivated speech act therefore functions like any other noun, even to the point of serving as a metaphor for something totally unrelated to a literal speech act ("l'*interjection* de fleurs," "comme une *vociféra-tion*"). Thus, if a performative utterance is originally a self-referential speech act, its production is simultaneously the production of a new referent into the world. This, however, is tantamount to a radical transformation of the notion of a referent, since, instead of pointing to an external object, language would then refer only to its own referring to itself in the act of referring, and the signifying chain would end in an infinitely self-duplicating loop. A variant of this difficulty has, in fact, been pointed out by Paul Larreya, who, in attempting to fit a performative utterance into a Chomskyan tree diagram, finds that "to develop the tree it would be necessary to repeat the symbol [designating the performative] an infinite number of times."[12] The performative utterance is thus the *mise en abyme* of reference itself.

We have now arrived at a predicament similar to that described by Richard Klein in his study of metaphors of metaphor,[13] but we are still a long way from showing what a poem has to say about the relation between this predicament and the characteristics of language in general. In pursuit of this question, let us examine some further implications of the self-referentiality of the performative utterance. If the performative refers only to itself, it would seem that it does not refer to any exterior

or prior origin. In actual analysis, however, we see that this is never considered to be the case. For although the sense and the reference of the
speech act are its own utterance, that very fact presupposes the presence of the utterer, who then becomes the necessary origin of the
speech act in question. Some sign of the speaker's presence to his
utterance is considered indispensable if the performative utterance is to
be what Austin calls "felicitous." But in this prose poem, the intentional continuity between the speaker and the utterance is being questioned
by the poet and his lady, for the "rêverie" that has been proclaimed to
the crowd "*s'ignore* et se lance nue de peur,*" just as the call to the
crowd to enter the booth in the first place had been "obscur pour moi-
même d'abord."[14] Indeed, if what the poet has spewed forth, "forcé,
sous le coup de poing brutal à l'estomac," can in any way be called
self-expression, it is so only in the etymological toothpaste-tube-like
sense of the word. The poem is not generated naturally by the poet's
subjective intentionality; it is, on the contrary, from the poet's mouth
untimely ripped. This, of course, is totally consistent with Mallarmé's
much-discussed elimination of the poetic subject: "L'oeuvre pure
implique la disparition élocutoire du poéte, qui cède l'initiative aux
mots. . . ."[15] Indeed, the active production of this discontinuity between the speaker and his words, far from eliminating the performative
dimension in Mallarmé's poetry, may itself constitute that poetry's
truly revolutionary performativity.

However, if we return now to how this elimination of subjectivity
is actually evoked at the end of *La Déclaration foraine,* we find that
even this formulation of the relation of speaker to speech is oversimplified. For the assertion of the nonintentionality of the poem is itself
so tortuously noncommittal that by the time it ends in an unequivocal
"c'est vrai," it has already practically qualified itself out of existence.
While naming the impatience of the crowd as the explicit "cause" only
of the figurative "punch in the stomach" that makes the poem "squirt
out" of the poet, the lady neither totally excludes the possibility of
the poem's having occurred in the carriage (into which the poet would
only "perhaps," "who knows?" not have introduced it), nor does she
articulate in any way the relation between punch and squirt, which
cannot even be said to meet on the same rhetorical level.

Turning to the circumstances surrounding the utterance of the one
true performative expression "je le gage," we find a similar problematization of the nature of the act performed. For if, according to Austin,
a bet can only be said to occur if it is accepted by a taker, the "peut-
être!" with which this taker "accepts" the poet's bet effectively suspends its application and thus its ability to function as a true act.

Moreover, what is or is not being wagered here seems itself internally inconsequent, since the "irrefutability" of the poet's spiel is dependent not on the clear univocality of its meaning, but, on the contrary, on the uncontrollable multiplicity of its repercussions.

Thus, while "c'est vrai" and "je le gage" explicitly mark the places of the constative and the performative respectively, what happens in between is that what is stated is the problematization of the conditions of performance, while what is wagered is the problematization of the possibility of statement.

Austin's theory, of course, contains no provision for this type of ambiguity. Its elimination is, in fact, one of the main motives behind the explicitation of a performative expression, since "the explicit performative rules out equivocation."[16] But behind the question of ambiguity, something much more unsettling is at stake, for it is not only equivocation that is ruled out by Austin's discussion of performative utterances: it is nothing less than poetry itself.

Splitting the Theoretical Hair

The points at which Austin dismisses poetry from his field of vision are frequent but usually parenthetical. One of these has been cited as our epigraph; the following is another:

> We could be issuing any of these utterances, as we can issue an utterance of any kind whatsoever, in the course, for example, of acting a play or making a joke or writing a poem—in which case of course it would not be seriously meant and we shall not be able to say that we seriously performed the act concerned. If the poet says "Go and catch a falling star" or whatever it may be, he doesn't seriously issue an order.[17]

The argument against poetry, theater, and jokes thus stems from the fact that the utterer's relation to his utterance is not "serious." He is not "seriously" doing what he would normally be doing in so uttering. But is this "etiolation" of language, as Austin dubs it elsewhere, a mere accident, a simple infelicity? Consider the example given: the poet says "Go and catch a falling star." In the context of Donne's poem, this order is not only not serious: it is explicitly impossible. It is a *rhetorical* imperative whose function, like that of a rhetorical question, is to elicit an impasse without naming it. The very nonseriousness of the order is in fact what constitutes its fundamental seriousness; if finding a faithful woman is like catching a falling star, according to Donne's poem, this is apparently very serious indeed.

But what about nonrhetorical poetic instances of performative expressions? When Virgil says "Arma virumque cano," is he not doing what he is saying? When Whitman says "I celebrate myself and sing myself," is this not a self-referential utterance? And when Pound asserts "I make a pact with you, Walt Whitman," does it really matter whether or not Whitman is listening? In affirming that "a performative utterance will be *in a peculiar way* hollow or void if said by an actor on the stage, or if introduced into a poem"[18] (emphasis in original), Austin is really objecting not to the use of the verb but to the status of its subject; in a poem, according to this argument, the intersubjective situation is fictionalized. The speaking subject is only a persona, an actor, not a person. But if one considers the conventionality of all performative utterances (on which Austin often insists), can it really be said that the chairman who opens a discussion or the priest who baptizes a baby or the judge who pronounces a verdict are persons rather than personae? This is precisely what Austin is admitting when he says "I do not take orders from you when you try to 'assert your authority' . . . on a desert island, as opposed to the case where you are the captain on a ship and therefore genuinely have authority."[19] The performative utterance thus automatically fictionalizes its utterer when it makes him the mouthpiece of a conventionalized authority. Where else, for example, but at a party *convention* could a presidential candidate be nominated? Behind the fiction of the subject stands the fiction of society,[20] for if one states that society began with a prohibition (of incest) or a (social) contract, one is simply stating that the origin of the authority behind a performative utterance is derived from a previous performative utterance whose ultimate origin is undeterminable. By using these *tu quoque* arguments, it is, of course, not our intention to nullify all differences between a poem and, say, a verdict, but only to problematize the assumptions on which such distinctions are based. If people are put to death by a verdict and not by a poem, it is not because the law is not a fiction.

The nonseriousness of a performative utterance "said by an actor on the stage" results, then, not from his fictional status but from his duality, from the spectator's consciousness that although the character in the play is swearing to avenge his dead father's ghost, the actor's own performative commitments lie elsewhere. But the performative utterance itself is here just as "serious" within the context of its surrounding fiction as it would be in the context of the fiction we call real life. Indeed, the question of seriousness attends the act of interpretation of *any* performative utterance. Rhetorical imperatives, for example, are far from being restricted to poetry; a large proportion of our ordinary conversational devices consists of such expressions as "Go jump in a lake," "Go fly a kite," and other more frequent but less mentionable retorts. The question of seriousness, far from marking the borders of the performative, is found to inhabit the very core of its territory. This is, in fact, one of the main factors behind Austin's recourse to the notion of illocutionary force. And this question, as it happens, is explicitly brought up by a line in our sonnet itself, to which we now turn:

> La chevelure vol d'une flamme à l'extrême
> Occident de désirs pour la tout déployer
> Se pose (je dirais mourir un diadème)
> Vers le front couronné son ancien foyer
>
> Mais sans or soupirer que cette vive nue
> L'ignition du feu toujours intérieur
> Originellement la seule continue
> Dans le joyau de l'oeil véridique ou rieur
>
> Une nudité de héros tendre diffame
> Celle qui ne mouvant astre ni feux au doigt
> Rien qu'à simplifier avec gloire la femme
> Accomplit par son chef fulgurante l'exploit
>
> De semer de rubis le doute qu'elle écorche
> Ainsi qu'une joyeuse et tutélaire torche.

The attempt to translate as many as possible of the ambiguities of this poem produces the following monstrosity, in which the reader is invited to choose only one of the boxed words at a time, but to accept all permutations of these choices that are grammatically possible. Punctuation may be added as needed.

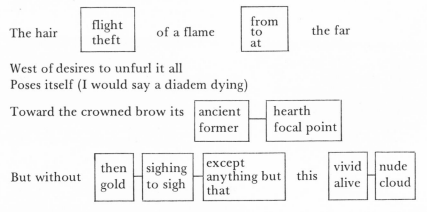

The hair [flight / theft] of a flame [from / to / at] the far
West of desires to unfurl it all
Poses itself (I would say a diadem dying)

Toward the crowned brow its [ancient / former] — [hearth / focal point]

But without [then / gold] [sighing / to sigh] — [except / anything but / that] this [vivid / alive] [nude / cloud]
The ignition of the always interior fire

Originally the only one [should continue / continues / that is continuous]

In the jewel of the truthful or laughing eye

| To extend a |
| A tender |

nudity of hero defames

The one who not moving star nor fires on her finger
Nothing but by simplifying with glory the woman
Accomplishes by her head, dazzling, the exploit

Of sowing with rubies the doubt she skins
Like a joyful and tutelary torch.

Here, it is the "oeil véridique ou rieur," roughly equivalent to the "naive or ironic reader," that raises the question of seriousness. By naming the problem of interpretation in terms of an alternative between seriousness and irony, the sonnet places itself between two incompatible readings of its own illocutionary force. Readers of *La Déclaration foraine* are indeed often sensitive to the mocking way in which the poet seems to treat his own creation; in her very helpful discussion of this prose poem, Ursula Franklin, for example, uses the word *irony* and its derivatives no less than fourteen times. But behind the question of illocutionary force lies the question of intentionality, which, as we have already seen, is here being subverted by the involuntary, blind relationship between the poet and his poem. We would therefore expect that the sonnet itself would somehow escape the simple dichotomy that it evokes between seriousness and irony as, indeed, the poet says it does when he speaks of its "compréhension multiple." Let us therefore examine the text of the poem in order to follow the precise functioning of this interpretative multiplicity.

This poem has been "read" many times.[21] There seems to be little doubt that it is "about" the woman standing behind it, and in particular, about her hair. But if one attempts to make explicit not the reference itself but the *sense* of the reference—what the poem is saying about the woman—one finds that the actual affirmations made by the poem are very difficult to pin down. In attempting to pursue even the simplest of interpretative strategies—the isolation of all the verbs in the present tense, for example—one stumbles over the word *continue,* which may be not a verb but an adjective and, even if it is a verb, may be either transitive or intransitive. But a tentative grammatical skeleton might run something like the following.

                    La chevelure
                    Se pose

                ⎧ Mais sans soupirer que cette nue continue dans
(choose one)   ⎨   le joyau de l'oeil
                ⎩ Mais sans rien soupirer (à l'exception de cette nue),
                       l'ignition du feu continue

                    Une nudité de héros diffame
                    Celle qui accomplit l'exploit

By teasing out three possible "declarations" from the reinsertion of this skeleton into the poem, we can conclude that the poem is saying that

1. The hair is just sitting there, but the lighting of the interior fire continues in the spectator's eye. The mere presence of the hero maligns this glorious simplification.

2. The hair sets itself down, but if the hero does not express the hope that this cloud (the fire or hair) continue in the spectator's eye, his tenderness maligns the lady.

3. The hair is posed. But, without gold, to sigh that this cloud extends the hero's naked tenderness to the spectator's eye is to malign the lady.

As if these affirmations were not already incompatible enough, the very word *diffamer* can be split into two diametrically opposed meanings; behind its ordinary performative sense of "to malign" stands the etymological, simple cognitive meaning "to reveal, divulge." The substitution of *reveal* for *malign* in our three readings effectively results not only in three more readings almost directly contrary to the original three, but in the passage from a performative to a constative function of those meanings.

This still oversimplified exposition of what the poem is saying should at least serve to demonstrate that the sonnet is talking less directly about the lady than about its relation to the lady. It is less about *something* than about *being about*. Simultaneously asserting both the necessity and the undesirability of its own existence, the poem refers to its own referring and not directly to its referent. But, it may be objected, is this not because that referent is itself so successfully "simplifying the Woman" that it does not need the poem? Is the lady's "exploit" not still being presented as a dazzlingly self-evident act in its own right? The poet's parting words to the crowd, indeed, appear to be saying just that.

> La personne qui a eu l'honneur de se soumettre à votre jugement, ne requiert pour vous communiquer le sens de son charme, un costume ou aucun accessoire usuel de théâtre. Ce naturel s'accommode de l'allusion parfaite que fournit la toilette toujours à l'un des motifs primordiaux de la femme, et suffit.
>
> [The person who has had the honor of submitting herself to your judgment, does not require in order to communicate to you the sense of her charm, a costume or any ordinary accessory of the theatre. This naturalness is accommodated by the perfect allusion furnished by a toilette always to one of the primordial motifs—or motives—of the woman, and suffices.]

Three hidden difficulties attend the reader who would take this explanation at face value. First, the meaning of "ce naturel" is ambiguous, since it refers back to the absence of theatrical accoutrements but forward to the allusive function of the lady's dress. "Ce naturel" becomes a central meaninglessness around which the presence and absence of allusions play. Second, this entire speech is introduced as "une *affectation* de retour à l'authenticité du spectacle," indicating that anyone who takes all this as the "meaning" of the sonnet—and almost every exegete has done so—is being taken in by a mere affectation. And third, the actual "exploit" referred to in the sonnet is not, as it is often misread, "simplifier la femme" but "semer de rubis le doute qu'elle écorche," the meaning of which is very far from being self-evident. The simplification of the woman is itself only an accessory to the highly problematic exploit of strewing rubies over a skinned doubt. Whatever this may mean, it is unlikely that it is an example of simple reference.

However, reference is not denied: it is problematized beyond reconciliation. The lady remains the referent of the poem, but only insofar as the poem says absolutely nothing about her. The moment she begins to stand for anything, including herself, she is no longer a referent but a sign. We can thus only see her as the poem's referent at the moment she ceases to be the poem's referent. This public display of (the lack of) that about which nothing can be said is described by Mallarmé elsewhere in similar terms:

> Jouant la partie, gratuitement soit pour un intérêt mineur: exposant notre Dame et Patronne à montrer sa déhiscence ou sa lacune, à l'égard de quelques rêves, comme la mesure à quoi tout se réduit.
>
> [Playing the game, gratuitously or for minor interest: exposing our Lady or Patroness to show her dehiscence or her lack, with respect to a number of dreams, as the measure to which all is reduced.]

If we now hazard a formulation of what the poem is saying, it would run something like this:

The hair *is,* but the poem's existence maligns and/or reveals the one who, by simplifying the Woman, accomplishes the act of aggravating and/or embellishing the uncertainty over the possibility and/or meaning of the poem's existence.

If this appears to be a reading that no reader in his right mind could possibly intuit, let alone accept, that is precisely the point. What is revolutionary in Mallarmé's poetics is less the elimination of the "object" than this very type of construction of a systematic set of self-emptying, nonintuitive meanings. Mallarmé's famous obscurity lies not in his devious befogging of the obvious but in his radical transformation of intelligibility itself through the ceaseless production of seemingly mutually exclusive readings of the same piece of language. *This* is what constitutes Mallarmé's break with referentiality, and not the simple abolition of the object, which would still be an entirely referential gesture. Reference is here not denied but suspended. The sonnet simultaneously takes on and discards meaning only to the extent that its contact with the lady's presence is contradictorily deferred. The "poème tu,"[22] the Book of *relations,* is not a simple absence of meaning; it is the systematic, dynamically self-subverting juxtaposition—*"rime"*[23] — of what becomes "true" only through its radical incompatibility with itself.

As we have seen, this "suspension" of meaning may occur through the simultaneous presence of contradictory affirmations. But if, as in the case of the word *diffame,* the play of contradictions lies in the very separation ("déhiscence") of a word from itself, this is a highly unsettling factor. The diachrony that has moved *diffamer* from the constative *divulge* to the performative *malign* is at work in any utterance whatsoever; quite apart from the question of seriousness, for example, the illocutionary force of an utterance is subject to the same kind of temporal fading and conventionalizing that produces "dead" metaphors and clichés. Benveniste's attempt to exclude "simple formulas" like "je m'excuse" and "bonjour" from consideration as "live" performatives is doomed by the very nature of "living" language itself.

That the logic of language renders some kind of discontinuity between speaker and speech absolutely inescapable is in fact demonstrated precisely by Austin's attempt to eliminate it. For the very word he uses to name "mere doing," the very name he gives to that from which he excludes theatricality, is none other than the word that most commonly *names* theatricality: the word *perform.* As if this were not ironic enough, exactly the same split can be found in Austin's other favorite word: *act.* How is it that a word that expresses most simply the mere doing of an act necessarily leads us to the question of—acting?

How is it possible to discuss the question of authenticity when that question already subverts the very terms we use to discuss it? Is it inevitable that the same split that divides the referent from itself the moment language comes near it should divide language from itself in the very same way? And can language actually refer to anything other than that very split? If Austin's unstated question was, What are we really *doing* when we speak? it becomes clear that, whatever else we may be doing, we are at any rate being "done in" by our own words. And it is precisely the unknowable extent to which our statement differs from itself that performs *us*. Decidedly, "leaving the initiative to words" is not as simple as it sounds. Left to their own initiative, the very words with which Austin excludes jokes, theater, and poetry from his field of vision inevitably take their revenge. But if, in the final analysis, the joke ends up being on Austin, it is, after all, only Poetic justice.

5. Poetry and Syntax: What the Gypsy Knew

Pivotal Intelligibility

Syntax is somehow not an inherently exciting subject. But without it, no subject would ever be capable of exciting us. Ever present but often taken for granted, like skin—which, as everyone knows, is a thing that when you have it outside, it helps keep your insides in—, syntax is a thing that when you have it in your surface structure, it helps keep your deep structure deep. But what happens when you examine syntax as such? What can be said about this necessary but insufficient condition for saying anything at all?

Faced with this question, I did what any modern student of poetics would do: I went to see what Mallarmé said about it. In his essay on the uses of obscurity, *Le Mystère dans les lettres* (*The Mystery in Letters*), Mallarmé writes:

> Quel pivot, j'entends, dans ces contrastes, à l'intelligibilité? il faut une garantie—
>
> La Syntaxe—[1]
>
> [What pivot, I understand, in these contrasts, for intelligibility?/A guarantee is needed—/Syntax—]

It should be noted that Mallarmé does not say that syntax guarantees intelligibility. He says it guarantees the *pivoting* of intelligibility. Intelligibility, indeed, is not an entirely positive value in Mallarmé's essay. It plays a role analogous to that of the word *entertainment* in today's discussions of art or pedagogy: it is a bone thrown to those who will never understand and a necessary evil or necessary tease for those who will. Mallarmé contrasts ordinary writers with the manipulator of

67

obscurity by saying that the former "puisent à quelque encrier sans Nuit la vaine couche suffisante d'intelligibilité que lui s'oblige, aussi, à observer, mais pas seule" ("draw from some Nightless inkwell the vain sufficient layer of intelligibility that he, too, obliges himself to observe, but not exclusively") (p. 383). Using an almost Chomskyan distinction between depth and surface, he explains:

> Tout écrit, extérieurement à son trésor, doit, par égard envers ceux dont il emprunte, après tout, pour un objet autre, le langage, présenter, avec les mots, un sens même indifférent: on gagne de détourner l'oisif, charmé que rien ne l'y concerne, à première vue.
>
> Salut, exact, de part et d'autre—
>
> Si, tout de même, n'inquiétait je ne sais quel *miroitement, en dessous,* peu séparable de la *surface* concédée à la rétine—il attire le soupçon: les malins, entre le public, réclamant de couper court, opinent, avec sérieux, que, juste, la teneur est inintelligible. (P. 382; emphasis mine here and passim)

> [Any piece of writing, outside of its treasures, ought, in deference to those from whom it borrows, after all, for a different purpose, language, to present, with words, a meaning however indifferent: one profits from thus turning away the idlers, charmed that nothing concerns them in it, at first sight.
>
> Greetings and just deserts on both sides—
>
> If, nevertheless, there were not I don't know what glimmering from underneath, hardly separable from the surface conceded to the retina—which awakens suspicion: the wise guys in the public, demanding that it be cut short, pronounce their seriously considered opinion that, precisely, the tenor is unintelligible.]

It is thus an obscure perception of the hidden possibility of obscurity that attracts the suspicions of the sly, casual reader, who would otherwise have been satisfied with whatever intelligibility the surface of the writing might present. Obscurity, in other words, is not encountered on the way to intelligibility, like an obstacle, but rather lies beyond it, as what prevents the reader from being satisfied with his own reading. Obscurity is an excess, not a deficiency, of meaning.

The poet does not seek to be unintelligible; his writing enacts the impossibility of a transparent, neutral style through its plays of depth and surface, darkness and light:

> Je partis d'intentions, comme on demande du style—neutre l'imagine-t-on—que son expression ne se fonce par le plongeon ni ne ruisselle d'éclaboussures jaillies: fermé à l'alternative qui est la loi. (P. 385)

> [I began with intentions as one demands of style—neutral style, one imagines—that its expression not plunge down into darkness nor surge up with a stream of splashes: closed to the alternative that is the law.]

The opposition between *plonger* (plunge) and *jaillir* (surge up) here merges with the opposition between darkness and light through the use of the verb *se foncer,* which means both "to become darker" and "to dive deeper." In going on to say, after speaking of "the alternative that is the law," that syntax acts as a pivot "in these contrasts," Mallarmé is making the very *fact of alternation* into the fundamental law of writing. Writing becomes an alternation between obscurity and clarity rather than a pursuit of either, a rhythm of intelligibility and mystery, just as time is a rhythm of days and nights:

> Ce procédé, jumeau, intellectuel, notable dans les symphonies, qui le trouvèrent au répertoire de la nature et du ciel. (P. 385)
>
> [This procedure, twin and intellectual, notable in symphonies, which found it in the repertory of nature and the sky.]

It should not be forgotten that day and night, *jour* and *nuit,* are in themselves examples of the law of simultaneous contradictory alternatives, since Mallarmé complains elsewhere that their sounds and their meanings are directly opposed:

> A côté d'*ombre,* opaque, *ténèbres* se fonce peu; quelle déception, devant la perversité conférant à *jour* comme à *nuit,* contradictoirement, des timbres obscur ici, là clair. Le souhait d'un terme de splendeur brillant, ou qu'il s'éteigne, inverse; quant à des alternatives lumineuses simples—*Seulement,* sachons *n'existerait pas le vers:* lui, philosophiquement rémunère le défaut des langues, complément supérieur. (P. 364; emphasis in original)
>
> [Alongside *ombre* [shade], which is opaque, *ténèbres* [shadows]   is   not particularly dark; what a disappointment to face the perversity that gives to *jour* [day] and *nuit* [night], contradictorily, a dark timbre here and a light one there. The hope of finding a term of splendor glowing, or else, inversely, being extinguished; as far as simple luminous alternatives are concerned—*Only,* let us note that *verse would not exist:* it is verse that philosophically compensates for the faults of languages, a superior complement.]

Verse, then, in its rhythms and rhymes, is a practice of pivoting, as its etymology (*versus*) indicates. It is an enactment of the alternative as law and of law as alternative, necessitated precisely by the perverse way language has of disappointing the search for simple alternatives. It is because language does *not* function as a perfect light meter, does not correspond to any "simple luminous alternatives," that constant alternation between clarity and obscurity becomes its law.

While pursuing this concept of syntax as a pivot for the turnings of darkness and light, I was startled to discover that the word *syntaxis* occurs in the title of a treatise by the second-century Greek astronomer, Ptolemy,[2] whose geocentric view of the relations among the bodies in the solar system also deals with the question of what in the world turns around what. Could Ptolemy's outmoded *Syntaxis* tell us anything about syntax and modern poetry? Is there a relation between grammar and gravitation? Could the relations between clarity and obscurity really be as simple—or as complex—as night and day?

The question Ptolemy's work mis-answers is, of course, the question of a center. Ptolemy saw the universe revolving around the earth; Copernicus saw the earth revolving around the sun in a universe in which the sun turns out to be merely one of many stars. The displacement of the center from earth to sun is also a movement away from the centrality of man himself; the human observer is no longer the pivot of the universe but only a parasite on a satellite. Freud, another revolutionizer of the status of man, compared his discovery of the unconscious precisely to a Copernican revolution. As Lacan puts it:

> "It was in fact the so-called Copernican revolution to which Freud himself compared his discovery, emphasizing that it was once again a question of the place man assigns to himself at the centre of a universe. . . . It is not a question of knowing whether I speak of myself in a way that conforms to what I am, but rather of knowing whether I am the same person as the one I am speaking of. . . . Is the place that I occupy as the subject of a signifier concentric or excentric, in relation to the place I occupy as subject of the signified?—That is the question."[3]

For Lacan, this psychoanalytical Copernican revolution takes place as a rewriting of the Cartesian *cogito*. Instead of "I think, therefore I am," we have: "I think where I am not, therefore I am where I do not think. . . . I am not wherever I am the plaything of my thought; I think of what I am where I do not think to think" (p. 166).

This mention of Descartes brings us back to the question of syntax, not only because Lacan has syntactically strung out the *cogito* but also because the modern theorist of the concept of syntax, Chomsky, is a self-proclaimed Cartesian. After contrasting the rationalist view of knowledge proposed by Descartes and Leibniz with the empiricist views proposed by Hume and the modern behaviorists, Chomsky writes of his own project: "A general linguistic theory of the sort described earlier . . . must . . . be regarded as a specific hypothesis, of an essentially rationalist cast, as to the nature of mental structures and processes."[4] But who is the syntaxer that will play Lacan to Chomsky's Descartes? Who is it that will revolutionize ratiocentric syntax?

The syntactical Copernicus we are seeking is, of course, none other than Mallarmé, who describes himself as "profondément et scrupuleusement syntaxier"[5] ("profoundly and scrupulously a syntaxer"), and whose *cogito* could be not "I think, therefore I am," but "I write, therefore I disappear." Mallarmé, although he is historically prior to

Chomsky, does indeed displace the verb-centered structures of Chomskyan grammars, putting a definitive crick in the syntax of what was once known as "la clarté française." In Mallarmé's syntax, there is often no central verb, or no verb at all, or a series of seemingly subordinate verbs with no main one. The sentences that conform to "le génie de la langue" are either semantically ambiguous or skeletons draped with conflicting interruptions. Mallarmé's syntax is never confused; it is, as he says, profound and scrupulous, as decentered as possible without being cut loose from the gravitational pull of incompatible grammatical possibilities.

Thus we can say that Mallarmé is to Chomsky as Copernicus is to Ptolemy as Freud is to Descartes, in that the former in each case works out a strategically rigorous decentering of the structure described by the latter, not by abandoning that structure but by multiplying the forces at work in the field of which that structure is a part. It is not by chance that Lacan, who makes much of Freud's discovery as a Copernican revolution, should also stylistically be one of the most important of Mallarmé's syntactic descendants. No one indeed in twentieth-century French literature is more "profondément et scrupuleusement syntaxier" than Lacan.

The Syntax of Assertion

> If you do know that *here is one hand*, we'll grant you all the rest.
>
> —Wittgenstein, *On Certainty*

In order to analyze further the implications of the Mallarméan revolution in syntax,[6] let us first consider two facets of Mallarmé's syntactic practices. While traditional syntax is what makes meaning decidable—what makes it impossible, for example, for "John kills Paul" to mean "Paul kills John"—, Mallarmé's syntax, as has often been noted, is precisely what makes the meaning of his poetry undecidable. In giving equal legitimacy to two contradictory syntactic arrangements in the same assertion,[7] Mallarmé renders the very nature of assertion problematic.

In Mallarmé's critical prose, where his syntactical revolution is carried out with equal precision, a second type of problematization of the status of assertion is often manifest. To take just one example, consider the following remarks about "literary art":

> Son sortilège, à lui, si ce n'est libérer, hors d'une poignée de poussière ou réalité sans l'enclore, au livre, même comme texte, la dispersion volatile soit l'esprit, qui n'a que faire de rien outre la musicalité de tout. (P. 645)

[Its spellbinding power, if it is not the liberation, out of a handful of dust or reality without enclosing it, in the book, even as a text, of the volatile dispersal, that is, the mind—which has to do with nothing outside the musicality of all.]

In violation of one of the most fundamental rules of syntax, there is no main verb in this passage. Where we might expect "son sortilège est," we find "son sortilège, si ce n'est." The verb *to be* has become hypothetical, negative, and subordinate. The syntax of the description of the relations between literature and the world withdraws it from the possibility of affirmation. In other words, what at first looks like a statement that literature disperses rather than states is *itself* dispersed, not stated. Instead of affirming that literature does not state, Mallarmé's syntax *enacts* the very incapacity to state which it is incapable of stating.

It is not by chance that the verb *to be* should be the verb Mallarmé most often skips or conjugates otherwise. What Mallarmé's syntactical revolution amounts to is a decentering of the epistemological or ontological functioning of language. The syntax of polyvalent, decentered, or failed assertion reveals the unreliability of language as a conveyer of anything other than the functioning of its own structure, which is perhaps what Mallarmé is here calling "la musicalité de tout." This does not mean that language speaks only about itself, but that it is incapable of *saying* exactly what it is *doing*.

In the wake of Mallarmé, twentieth-century poetry has questioned the nature and possibility of assertion in a number of other ways. In surrealistic or automatic writing, effects of strangeness are often achieved by replacing normal semantic associations with bizarre incompatibilities within a syntax that remains relatively intact. "The earth is blue like an orange," for example, can only achieve its flash of impossibility through the tranquil assertiveness of its structure. Another modern phenomenon, pictorial or concrete poetry, suspends the syntax of assertion by transferring the reader's attention from the content of the signified to the typographical syntax of the signifier. It is through these and other poetic procedures that modern poetry makes explicit the problematizations enacted in Mallarmé's syntax. But must an assertion be—syntactically or semantically—manhandled in order to be problematic? Is there not something intrinsically enigmatic about the act of asserting as such?

All discourses, including poetry, make assertions. Assertions create referential effects. To assert is to appear to know, even if it is a knowledge of doubt. It would seem that the structure of knowledge and the syntax of assertion are inseparable. But it also seems necessary to cling to the belief that it makes a difference which comes first; the ground of everything seems to shift if we consider knowledge as an effect of language instead of language as an effect of knowledge.

The Swiss psychologist Jean Piaget, whose views of the development of operational thought in many ways parallel Chomskyan linguistics, concludes on the basis of certain tests that syntax acquisition in children can only occur when cognitive development is ready for it. He writes that "language serves to translate what is already understood. . . . The level of understanding seems to modify the language used rather than vice versa."[8] While experimental science here seems to believe that syntax follows and translates prior understanding, I would like now to analyze how literature can be seen to say neither this nor the opposite, but to dramatize something quite different about the relations between syntax and knowledge. I shall turn to a poem by Apollinaire, "La Tzigane," in which obvious syntactic signals of the problematization of assertion are conspicuously absent:

La Tzigane

La tzigane savait d'avance
Nos deux vies barrées par les nuits
Nous lui dîmes adieu et puis
De ce puits sortit l'Espérance

L'amour lourd comme un ours privé
Dansa debout quand nous voulûmes
Et l'oiseau bleu perdit ses plumes
Et les mendiants leurs *Ave*

On sait bien que l'on se damne
Mais l'espoir d'aimer en chemin
Nous fait penser main dans la main
A ce qu'a prédit la tzigane[9]

[*The Gypsy.* The gypsy knew in advance/ Our two lives crossed by nights/ We told her farewell and then/ Out of that well sprang hope // Love as heavy as a private bear / Danced upright whenever we wanted / And the blue bird lost its feathers/ And the beggars their *Ave*'s // Everyone knows that we are damned/ But the hope of loving along the way/ Makes us think, hand in hand,/ Of what the gypsy once foretold.]

The assertiveness of this poem is reinforced by the repetition of the verb *savoir* ("to know"): the poem begins with "La tzigane savait d'avance" and ends with "on sait bien." But what is the content of this knowledge? What is the poem affirming? In the first sentence—"La tzigane savait d'avance/ Nos deux vies barrées par les nuits"—what the gypsy knew is not immediately intelligible. "Nos deux vies barrées par les nuits" could mean "our lives crisscrossed by nights of love," "our lives crossed out by darknesses," "our lives fettered by intimations of mortality," or "our lives ruined by our love." The prophecy would seem to be readable both positively and negatively, both as a prediction of love and as a prediction of loss. In the last stanza, the sentence "On sait bien que l'on se damne" reinforces the negative reading, yet in pivoting on a *mais*—"Mais l'espoir d'aimer en chemin/Nous fait penser main dans la main/A ce qu'a prédit la tzigane"—the poem returns to the gypsy's prediction in *opposition* to damnation. What then did the gypsy actually know? The answer seems both indicated and refused by the ambiguous word *barrées. Barrer,* which means both "to mark" and "to block," has thus itself marked out and blocked our very attempt to interpret the poem. The word *barré,* in other words, is enacting its meaning in its very refusal to mean. It is as though Apollinaire had made our interpretation turn on a crossed-out word instead of a word meaning "crossed out."

But this effectively displaces the poem's center of gravity. Instead of recounting the *content* of a prediction, the poem is recounting the *effects* of a prediction the content of which is never clear. The reader, like the consulters of the gypsy, is fooled into thinking he has been told something that can then turn out to be true or false. The syntax of affirmation causes him to forget that he has not really been told anything at all. If the gypsy's prediction is derived from a reading of the lines of the hand—which is also perhaps suggested by *barré*—then the final image of thinking of the gypsy while walking hand in hand, which casts the lines of the hand into total darkness, indicates that the message has become dark precisely because it has been embraced.

The fact of the gypsy's prediction, therefore, acts as the syntactical overdetermination of an unintelligible meaning that produces the same effects as knowledge. Life, love, death, happiness, deprivation, and damnation here revolve around the *syntax* of knowledge, not around knowledge itself. The same assertiveness that preserves outmoded knowledge in Ptolemy's writing produces anticipatory knowledge not in the gypsy but in her readers. Here, reading is believing that something has been predicted, as the poem's third and fourth lines suggest:

Nous lui dîmes adieu et puis
De ce puits sortit l'Espérance.

It is out of the well ("puits") of anticipation ("puis") that the hope of understanding arises. The juxtaposition of the homonyms *puits* and *puis* can be read as a figure for the relations between the syntactical and the semantic functions in the poem. The well is a traditional image for the locus of truth, for depth of meaning, while the linear, temporal seriality of syntax can be represented by the expression "and then." If the well of meaning is here bottomless, however, it is precisely because of its syntactical overdetermination: the *puits* of sense is both produced and emptied by the *puis* of syntax.

Thus, it is not the gypsy that knows in advance, but the syntax of assertion that is always in advance of knowledge. Knowledge is nothing other than an effect of syntax, not merely because any affirmation creates an illusion of knowledge, but precisely because syntax is what makes it possible for us to treat as *known* anything that we do not *know* we do not know. And this, in one form or another, is what poetry has always known.

PART THREE:
DIFFERENCE
IN THE ACT

6. Melville's Fist:
The Execution of *Billy Budd*

The Sense of an Ending

> Truth uncompromisingly told will always have its ragged edges; hence the conclusion of such a narration is apt to be less finished than an architectural finial.
> —Melville, *Billy Budd*

The plot of Melville's *Billy Budd* is well known, and, like its title character, appears entirely straightforward and simple. It is a tale of three men in a boat: the innocent, ignorant foretopman, handsome Billy Budd; the devious, urbane master-at-arms, John Claggart; and the respectable, bookish commanding officer, Captain the Honorable Edward Fairfax ("Starry") Vere. Falsely accused by Claggart of plotting mutiny aboard the British man-of-war *Bellipotent*, Billy Budd, his speech impeded by a stutter, strikes his accuser dead in front of the captain, and is condemned, after a summary trial, to hang.

In spite of the apparent straightforwardness of the facts of the case, however, there exists in the critical literature on *Billy Budd* a notable range of disagreement over the ultimate meaning of the tale. For some, the story constitutes Melville's "testament of acceptance," his "everlasting yea," his "acceptance of tragedy," or at least his "recognition of necessity."[1] For others, Melville's "final stage" is, on the contrary, "irony": *Billy Budd* is considered a "testament of resistance," "ironic social criticism," or the last vituperation in Melville's "quarrel with God."[2] More recently, critical attention has devoted itself to the ambiguity in the story, sometimes deploring it, sometimes revelling in it, and sometimes simply listing it.[3] The ambiguity is attributed to various causes: the unfinished state of the manuscript, Melville's change of heart toward Vere, Melville's unreconciled ambivalence

toward authority or his guilt about paternity, the incompatibility between the "plot" and the "story."[4] But however great the disagreement
over the meaning of this posthumous novel, all critics seem to agree in
considering it Melville's "last word." "With the mere fact of the long
silence in our minds," writes John Middleton Murry, "we could not
help regarding 'Billy Budd' as the last will and spiritual testament of a
man of genius."[5]

To regard a story as its author's last will and testament is clearly to
grant it a privileged, determining position in the body of that author's
work. As its name implies, the "will" is taken to represent the author's
final "intentions": in writing his will, the author is presumed to have
summed up and evaluated his entire literary output, and directed it—as
proof against "dissemination"—toward some determinable destination.
The "ending" thus somehow acquires the metalinguistic authority to
confer finality and intelligibility upon all that precedes it.

Now, since this sense of Melville's ending is so central to *Billy Budd*
criticism, it might be useful to take a look at the nature of the ending
of the story itself. Curiously enough, we find that *Billy Budd* ends not
once, but no less than four times. As Melville himself describes it, the
story continues far beyond its "proper" end: "How it fared with the
Handsome Sailor during the year of the Great Mutiny has been faithfully given. But though *properly* the story ends with his life, something
in the way of sequel will not be amiss"[6] (emphasis mine here and passim).
This "sequel" consists of "three brief chapters": (1) the story of the
death of Captain Vere after an encounter with the French ship, the
Athée; (2) a transcription of the Budd-Claggart affair published in an
"authorized" naval publication, in which the characters of the two men
are reversed, with Budd represented as the depraved villain and Claggart
as the heroic victim; and (3) a description of the posthumous mythifi-
cation of Billy Budd by his fellow sailors and a transcription of the
ballad written by one of them, which presents itself as a monologue
spoken by Billy on the eve of his execution. Billy Budd's last words,
like Melville's own, are thus spoken posthumously—indeed the final
line of the story is uttered from the bottom of the sea.

The question of the sense of Melville's ending is thus raised *in* the
story as well as *by* the story. But far from tying up the loose ends of a
confusing literary life, Melville's last words are an affirmation of the
necessity of "ragged edges":

> The symmetry of form attainable in pure fiction cannot so readily be achieved
> in a narration essentially having less to do with fable than with fact. Truth un-
> compromisingly told will always have its ragged edges; hence the conclusion of
> such a narration is apt to be less finished than an architectural finial. (P. 405)

The story ends by fearlessly fraying its own symmetry, thrice trans-gressing its own "proper" end; there is something inherently improper about this testimentary disposition of Melville's literary property. In-deed, far from totalizing itself into intentional finality, the story in fact begins to repeat itself—retelling itself first in reverse, and then in verse. The ending not only lacks special authority, it problematizes the very *idea* of authority by placing its own reversal in the pages of an "authorized" naval chronicle. To end is to repeat, and to repeat is to be ungovernably open to revision, displacement, and reversal.[7] The sense of Melville's ending is to empty the ending of any privileged control over sense.

The Plot against the Characters

> For Tragedy is an imitation, not of men, but of action and of life, and life con-sists in action, and its end is a mode of action, not a quality. Now character determines men's qualities, but it is by their actions that they are happy or the reverse.
>
> —Aristotle, *Poetics*

In beginning our study of *Billy Budd* with its ending, we, too, seem to have reversed the "proper" order of things. Most studies of the story tend to begin, after a few general remarks about the nature of good and evil, with a delineation of the three main characters: Billy, Claggart, and Vere. As Charles Weir puts it, "The purely physical ac-tion of the story is clear enough, and about its significant details there is never any doubt. . . . It is, therefore, with some consideration of the characters of the three principal actors that any analysis must begin."[8] "Structurally," writes F. B. Freeman, "the three characters *are* the novel"[9] (emphasis in original).

Melville goes to great lengths to describe both the physical and the moral characteristics of his protagonists. Billy Budd, a twenty-one-year-old "novice in the complexities of factitious life," is remarkable for his "significant personal beauty," "reposeful good nature," "straight-forward simplicity" and "unconventional rectitude." But Billy's in-telligence ("such as it was," says Melville) is as primitive as his virtues are pristine. He is illiterate, he cannot understand ambiguity, and he stutters.

Claggart, on the other hand, is presented as the very image of ur-bane, intellectualized, articulate evil. Although "of no ill figure upon the whole" (p. 342), something in Claggart's pallid face consistently inspires uneasiness and mistrust. He is a man, writes Melville, "in whom was the mania of an evil nature, not engendered by vicious training or corrupting books or licentious living, but born with him and innate, in short, 'a depravity according to nature'" (p. 354). The mere sight of Billy Budd's rosy beauty and rollicking innocence does not fail to provoke in such a character "an antipathy spontaneous and profound" (p. 351).

The third man in the drama, who has inspired the greatest critical dissent, is presented in less vivid but curiously more contradictory terms. The *Bellipotent*'s captain is described as both unaffected and pedantic, dreamy and resolute, irascible and undemonstrative, "mindful of the welfare of his men, but never tolerating an infraction of discipline," "intrepid to the verge of temerity, though never injudiciously so" (p. 338). While Billy and Claggart are said to owe their characters to "nature," Captain Vere is shaped mainly by his fondness for books:

> He loved books, never going to sea without a newly replenished library, compact but of the best. . . . With nothing of that literary taste which less heeds the thing conveyed than the vehicle, his bias was toward those books to which every serious mind of superior order occupying any active post of authority in the world naturally inclines: books treating of actual men and events no matter of what era—history, biography, and unconventional writers like Montaigne, who, free from cant and convention, honestly and in the spirit of common sense philosophize upon realities. (P. 340)

Vere, then, is an honest, serious reader, seemingly well suited for the role of judge and witness that in the course of the story he will come to play.

No consideration of the nature of character in *Billy Budd,* however, can fail to take into account the fact that the fate of each of the characters is the direct reverse of what one is led to expect from his "nature." Billy is sweet, innocent, and harmless, yet he kills. Claggart is evil, perverted, and mendacious, yet he dies a victim. Vere is sagacious and responsible, yet he allows a man whom he feels to be blameless to hang. It is this discrepancy between character and action that gives rise to the critical disagreement over the story: readers tend either to save the plot and condemn Billy ("acceptance," "tragedy," or "necessity"), or to save Billy and condemn the plot ("irony," "injustice," or "social criticism").

In an effort to make sense of this troubling incompatibility between character and plot, many readers are tempted to say of Billy and Claggart, as does William York Tindall, that "each is more important for what he is than what he does. . . . Good and bad, they occupy the region of good and evil."[10] This reading effectively preserves the allegori-

cal values suggested by Melville's opening chapters, but it does so only
by denying the importance of the plot. It ends where the plot begins:
with the identification of the moral natures of the characters. One may
therefore ask whether the allegorical interpretation (good vs. evil) depends as such on this sort of preference for being over doing, and if so,
what effect the incompatibility between character and action may have
on the allegorical functioning of *Billy Budd.*

Interestingly enough, Melville both invites an allegorical reading
and subverts the very terms of its consistency when he writes of the
murder: "Innocence and guilt personified in Claggart and Budd in effect changed places" (p. 380). Allowing for the existence of personification but reversing the relation between personifier and personified,
positioning an opposition between good and evil only to make each
term take on the properties of its opposite, Melville sets up his plot in
the form of a chiasmus:

This story, which is often read as a retelling of the story of Christ, is
thus literally a cruci-fiction—a fiction structured in the shape of a cross.
At the moment of the reversal, an instant before his fist shoots out,
Billy's face seems to mark out the point of crossing, bearing "an expression which was as a crucifixion to behold" (p. 376). Innocence and
guilt, criminal and victim, change places through the mute expressive-
ness of Billy's inability to speak.

If *Billy Budd* is indeed an allegory, it is an allegory of the questioning of the traditional conditions of allegorical stability. The requirement
of Melville's plot that the good act out the evil designs of the bad while
the bad suffer the unwarranted fate of the good indicates that the real
opposition with which Melville is preoccupied here is less the static
opposition between evil and good than the dynamic opposition between a man's "nature" and his acts, or, in Tindall's terms, the relation
between human "being" and human "doing."

Curiously enough, it is precisely this question of being versus doing
that is brought up by the only sentence we ever see Claggart directly
address to Billy Budd. When Billy accidentally spills his soup across the
path of the master-at-arms, Claggart playfully replies, "Handsomely
done, my lad! And handsome *is* as handsome *did* it, too!" (p. 350).
The proverbial expression "handsome is as handsome does," from
which this exclamation springs, posits the possibility of a continuous,
predictable, transparent relationship between being and doing. It

supposes that the inner goodness of Billy Budd is in harmonious accord with his fair appearance, that, as Melville writes of the stereotypical "Handsome Sailor" in the opening pages of the story, "the moral nature" is not "out of keeping with the physical make" (p. 322). But it is this very continuity between the physical and the moral, between appearance and action, or between being and doing, that Claggart questions in Billy Budd. He warns Captain Vere not to be taken in by Billy's physical beauty: "You have but noted his fair cheek. A mantrap may be under the ruddy-tipped daisies" (p. 372). Claggart indeed soon finds his suspicions confirmed with a vengeance: when he repeats his accusation in front of Billy, the master-at-arms is struck down dead. It would thus seem that to question the continuity between character and action cannot be done with impunity, that fundamental questions of life and death are always surreptitiously involved.

In an effort to examine what is at stake in Claggart's accusation, it might be helpful to view the opposition between Billy and Claggart as an opposition not between innocence and guilt but between two conceptions of language, or between two types of reading. Billy seemingly represents the perfectly *motivated* sign; that is, his inner self (the signified) is considered transparently readable from the beauty of his outer self (the signifier). His "straightforward simplicity" is the very opposite of the "moral obliquities" or "crookedness of heart" that characterize "citified" or rhetorically sophisticated man. "To deal in double meanings and insinuations of any sort," writes Melville, "was quite foreign to his nature" (p. 327). In accordance with his "nature," Billy reads everything at face value, never questioning the meaning of appearances. He is dumbfounded at the Dansker's suggestion, "incomprehensible to a novice," that Claggart's very pleasantness can be interpreted as its opposite, as a sign that he is "down on" Billy Budd. To Billy, "the occasional frank air and pleasant word *went for what they purported to be,* the young sailor never having heard as yet of the 'too fair-spoken man'" (pp. 365–66). As a reader, then, Billy is symbolically as well as factually illiterate. His literal-mindedness is represented by his illiteracy because, in assuming that language can be taken at face value, he excludes the very functioning of *difference* that makes the act of reading both indispensable and undecidable.

Claggart, on the other hand, is the image of difference and duplicity, both in his appearance and in his character. His face is not ugly, but it hints of something defective or abnormal. He has no vices, yet he incarnates evil. He is an intellectual, but uses reason as "an ambidexter implement for effecting the irrational" (p. 354). Billy inspires in him both "profound antipathy" and "soft yearning." In the incompatibility of his attributes, Claggart is thus a personification of ambiguity and ambivalence, of the distance between signifier and signified, of the separation between being and doing: "apprehending the good, but powerless to be it, a nature like Claggart's . . . what recourse is left to it but to recoil upon itself" (p. 356). As a reader, Claggart has learned to "exercise a distrust keen in proportion to the fairness of the appearance" (p. 364). He is properly an ironic reader, who, assuming the sign to be arbitrary and unmotivated, reverses the value signs of appearances and takes a daisy for a mantrap and an unmotivated accidental spilling of soup for an intentional, sly escape of antipathy. Claggart meets his downfall, however, when he attempts to master the arbitrariness of the sign for his own ends by falsely (that is, arbitrarily) accusing Billy of harboring arbitrariness, of hiding a mutineer beneath the appearance of a baby.

Such a formulation of the Budd/Claggart relationship enables one to take a new look not only at the story itself but at the criticism as well. For this opposition between the literal reader (Billy) and the ironic reader (Claggart) is reenacted in the critical readings of *Billy Budd* in the opposition between the "acceptance" school and the "irony" school. Those who see the story as a "testament of acceptance" tend to take Billy's final benediction of Vere at face value; as Lewis Mumford puts it, "As Melville's own end approached, he cried out with Billy Budd: God Bless Captain Vere! In this final affirmation Herman Melville died."[11] In contrast, those who read the tale ironically tend to take Billy's sweet farewell as Melville's bitter curse. Joseph Schiffman writes, "At heart a kind man, Vere, strange to say, makes possible the depraved Claggart's wish—the destruction of Billy. 'God bless Captain Vere!' Is this not piercing irony? As innocent Billy utters these words, does not the reader gag?"[12] But since the acceptance/irony dichotomy is already contained within the story, since it is obviously one of the things the story is *about,* it is not enough to try to decide which of the readings is correct. What the reader of *Billy Budd* must do is to analyze what is at stake in the very opposition between literality and irony. This question, crucial for an understanding of *Billy Budd* not only as a literary but also as a critical phenomenon, will be taken up again in the final pages of the present chapter, but first let us examine further the linguistic implications of the murder itself.

The Fiend That Lies Like Truth

> Outwardly regarded, our craft is a lie; for all that is outwardly seen of it is the clean-swept deck, and oft-painted planks comprised above the water-line;

whereas, the vast mass of our fabric, with all its store-rooms of secrets, forever
slides along far under the surface.

—Melville, *White-Jacket*

If Claggart's accusation that Billy is secretly plotting mutiny is essentially an affirmation of the possibility of a discontinuity between
being and doing, of an arbitrary, nonmotivated relation between signifier and signified, then Billy's blow must be read as an attempt violently
to deny that discontinuity or arbitrariness. The blow, as a denial, functions as a substitute for speech, as Billy explains during his trial: "I did
not mean to kill him. Could I have used my tongue I would not have
struck him. But he foully lied to my face and in presence of my captain, and I had to say something, and I could only say it with a blow"
(p. 383). But in striking a blow in defense of the sign's motivation,
Billy actually personifies the very *absence* of motivation: "I did not
mean . . ." His blow is involuntary, accidental, properly unmotivated.
He is a sign that does not mean to mean. Billy, who cannot understand
ambiguity, who takes pleasant words at face value and then obliterates
Claggart for suggesting that one could do otherwise, whose sudden blow
is a violent denial of any discrepancy between his being and his doing,
ends up radically illustrating the very discrepancy he denies.

The story thus takes place between the postulate of continuity between signifier and signified ("handsome is as handsome does") and
the postulate of their discontinuity ("a mantrap may be under the
ruddy-tipped daisies"). Claggart, whose accusations of incipient mutiny
are apparently false and therefore illustrate the very double-facedness
that they attribute to Billy, is negated for proclaiming the lie about
Billy which Billy's act of negation paradoxically proves to be the truth.

This paradox can also be stated in another way, in terms of the
opposition between the performative and the constative functions of
language. Constative language is language used as an instrument of
cognition—it describes, reports, speaks *about* something other than
itself. Performative language is language that itself functions as an act,
not as a report of one. Promising, betting, swearing, marrying, and
declaring war, for example, are not descriptions of acts but acts in their
own right. The proverb "handsome is as handsome does" can thus also
be read as a statement of the compatibility between the constative
(being) and the performative (doing) dimensions of language. But what
Billy's act dramatizes is their radical *incompatibility*—Billy performs
the truth of Claggart's report to Vere only by means of his absolute
and blind denial of its cognitive validity. If Billy had understood the
truth, he would not have performed it. Handsome cannot both be and

do its own undoing. The knowledge that being and doing are incompatible cannot know the ultimate performance of its own confirmation.

Melville's chiasmus thus creates a reversal not only of the places of guilt and innocence but also of the postulate of continuity and the postulate of discontinuity between doing and being, performance and cognition. When Billy's fist strikes Claggart's forehead, it is no longer possible for knowing and doing to meet. Melville's story does not report the occurence of a particularly deadly performative utterance, the tale itself performs the radical incompatibility between knowledge and acts.

All this, we recall, is triggered by a stutter, a linguistic defect. No analysis of the story's dramatization of linguistic categories can be complete without careful attention to this glaring infelicity. Billy's "vocal defect" is presented and explained in the story in the following terms:

> There was just one thing amiss in him . . . an occasional liability to a vocal defect. Though in the hour of elemental uproar or peril he was everything that a sailor should be, yet under sudden provocation of strong heart-feeling his voice, otherwise singularly musical, as if expressive of the harmony within, was apt to develop an organic hesitancy, in fact more or less of a stutter or even worse. In this particular Billy was a striking instance that the arch interferer, the envious marplot of Eden, still has more or less to do with every human consignment to this planet of Earth. In every case, one way or another he is sure to slip in his little card, as much as to remind us—I too have a hand here. (Pp. 331–32)

It is doubtless this satanic "hand" that shoots out when Billy's speech fails him. Billy is all too literally a "*striking* instance" of the workings of the "envious marplot."

Melville's choice of the word *marplot* to characterize the originator of Billy's stutter deserves special note. It seems logical to understand that the stutter "mars" the plot in that it triggers the reversal of roles between Billy and Claggart. Yet in another sense this reversal does not mar the plot, it constitutes it. Here, as in the story of Eden, what the envious marplot mars is not the plot, but the state of plotlessness that exists "in the beginning." What both the Book of Genesis and *Billy Budd* narrate is thus not the story of a fall, but a fall into story.

In this connection, it is relevant to recall that Claggart falsely accuses Billy of instigating a *plot,* of stirring up mutiny against the naval authorities. What Claggart is in a sense doing by positing this fictitious plot is trying desperately to scare up a plot for the story. And it is Billy's very act of denial of his involvement in any plot that finally brings him *into* the plot. Billy's involuntary blow is an act of mutiny not only against the authority of his naval superiors but also against the authority of his own conscious intentions. Perhaps it is not by chance that the word *plot* can mean both "intrigue" and "story". If all plots somehow tell the story of their own marring, then perhaps it could be said that all plots are plots against authority, that authority creates the scene of its own destruction, that all stories necessarily recount by their very existence the subversion of the father, of the gods, of consciousness, of order, of expectations, or of meaning.

But is Billy truly as "plotless" as he appears? Does his "simplicity" hide no division, no ambiguity? As many critics have remarked, Billy's character seems to result mainly from his exclusion of the negative. When informed that he is being arbitrarily impressed for service on a man-of-war, Billy "makes no demur" (p. 323). When invited to a clandestine meeting by a mysterious stranger, Billy acquiesces through his "incapacity of plumply saying *no*" (p. 359, emphasis in original). But it is interesting to note that although Billy thus seems to be "just a boy who cain't say no," almost all the words used to describe him are negative in form: innocent, unconventional, illiterate, unsophisticated, unadulterate, etc. And although he denies any discrepency between what is said and what is meant, he does not prove to be totally incapable of lying. When asked about the shady visit of the afterguardsman, he distorts his account in order to edit out anything that indicates any incompatibility with the absolute maintenance of authority. He neglects to report the questionable proposition even though "it was his duty as a loyal bluejacket" (p. 362) to do so. In thus shrinking from "the dirty work of a telltale" (p. 362), Billy maintains his "plotlessness" not spontaneously but through a complex act of filtering. Far from being simply and naturally pure, he is obsessed with maintaining his own irreproachability in the eyes of authority. After witnessing a flogging, he is so horrified that he resolves "that never through remissness would he make himself liable to such a visitation or do or omit aught that might merit even verbal reproof" (p. 346). Billy does not simply exclude the negative; he represses it. His reaction to questionable behavior of any sort (such as that of Red Whiskers, the afterguardsman, Claggart) is to obliterate it. He retains his "*blank* ignorance" (p. 363) only by a vigorous act of erasing. As Melville says of Billy's reaction to Claggart's petty provocations, "the ineffectual speculations into which he was led were so disturbingly alien to him that *he did his best to smother them*" (p. 362).

In his *disgustful recoil* from an overture which, though he but ill comprehended, he *instinctively knew* must involve evil of some sort, Billy Budd was like a young horse fresh from the pasture suddenly inhaling a vile whiff from some chemical factory, and by repeated snortings trying to *get it out* of his

nostrils and lungs. This frame of mind *barred all desire* of holding further par-
ley with the fellow, even were it but for the purpose of gaining some enlighten-
ment as to his design in approaching him. (P. 361)

Billy maintains his purity only through constant, though unconscious,
censorship. "Innocence," writes Melville, "was his blinder" (p. 366).

It is interesting to note that while the majority of readers see Billy
as a personification of goodness and Claggart as a personification of
evil, those who do not, tend to read from a psychoanalytical point of
view. Much has been made of Claggart's latent homosexuality, which
Melville clearly suggests. Claggart, like the hypothetical "X—," "is a
nut not to be cracked by the tap of a lady's fan" (p. 352). The "unob-
served glance" he sometimes casts upon Billy contains "a touch of soft
yearning, as if Claggart could even have loved Billy but for fate and
ban" (p. 365). The spilling of the soup and Claggart's reaction to it are
often read symbolically as a sexual exchange, the import of which, of
course, is lost on Billy, who cannot read.

According to this perspective, Claggart's so-called evil is thus really
a repressed form of love. But it is perhaps even more interesting to examine the way in which the psychoanalytical view treats Billy's so-
called goodness as being in reality a repressed form of hate:

> The persistent feminine imagery . . . indicate[s] that Billy has identified him-
> self with the mother at a pre-Oedipean level and has adopted the attitude of
> harmlessness and placation toward the father in order to avoid the hard strug-
> gle of the Oedipus conflict. . . . That all Billy's rage and hostility against the
> father are unconscious is symbolized by the fact that whenever aroused it can-
> not find expression in spoken language. . . . This is a mechanism for keeping
> himself from admitting his own guilt and his own destructiveness.[13]

> All of Billy's conscious acts are toward passivity. . . . In symbolic language,
> Billy Budd is seeking his own castration—seeking to yield up his vitality to an
> authoritative but kindly father, whom he finds in Captain Vere.[14]

> Quite often a patient begins to stutter when he is particularly eager to prove a
> point. Behind his apparent zeal he has concealed a hostile or sadistic tendency
> to destroy his opponent by means of words, and the stuttering is both a block-
> ing of and a punishment for this tendency. Still more often stuttering is exacer-
> bated by the presence of prominent or authoritative persons, that is, of
> paternal figures against whom the unconscious hostility is most intense.[15]

> Although *Billy Budd, Sailor* is placed in historical time . . . the warfare is not
> between nations for supremacy on the seas but between father and son in the
> eternal warfare to determine succession.[16]

> When Vere becomes the father, Claggart and Billy are no longer sailors but sons
> in rivalry for his favor and blessing. Claggart manifestly is charging mutiny but
> latently is accusing the younger son or brother of plotting the father's over-
> throw. . . . When Billy strikes Claggart with a furious blow to the forehead, he

puts out the "evil eye" of his enemy-rival, but at the same time the blow is displaced, since Billy is prohibited from striking the father. After Claggart is struck and lies on the deck "a dead snake," Vere covers his face in silent recognition of the displaced blow.[17]

Billy's type of innocence is . . . *pseudoinnocence*. . . . Capitalizing on naiveté, it consists of a childhood that is never outgrown, a kind of fixation on the past. . . . When we face questions too big and too horrendous to contemplate . . . we tend to shrink into this kind of innocence and make a virtue of powerlessness, weakness, and helplessness. . . . It is this innocence that cannot come to terms with the destructiveness in one's self or others; and hence, as with Billy Budd, it actually becomes self-destructive.[18]

The psychoanalytical reading is thus a demystification of the notion of innocence portrayed in *Billy Budd*. In the psychoanalytical view, what underlies the metaphysical lament that in this world "goodness is impotent" is the idea that impotence is good, that harmlessness is innocent, that naiveté is lovable, that "giving no cause of offense to anybody" and resolving never "to do or omit aught that might merit . . . reproof" (p. 346) are the highest ideals in human conduct. While most readers react to Billy as do his fellow crew-members ("they all love him," [p. 325]), the psychoanalysts share Claggart's distrust ("for all his youth and good looks, a deep one," [p. 371]) and even disdain ("to be nothing more than innocent!" [p. 356]).

In this connection it is curious to note that while the psychoanalysts have implicitly chosen to adopt the attitude of Claggart, Melville, in the crucial confrontation scene, comes close to presenting Claggart as a psychoanalyst:

With the measured step and calm collected air of an asylum physician approaching in the public hall some patient beginning to show indications of a coming paroxysm, Claggart deliberately advanced within short range of Billy, and, mesmerically looking him in the eye, briefly recapitulated the accusation. (p. 375).

It is as though Claggart as analyst, in attempting to bring Billy's unconscious hostility to consciousness, unintentionally unleashes the destructive acting-out of transferential rage. The fatal blow, far from being an unmotivated accident, is the gigantic return of the power of negation that Billy has been repressing all his life. And in his blind destructiveness, Billy lashes out against the "father" as well as against the very process of analysis itself.

The difference between the psychoanalytical and the traditional "metaphysical" readings of *Billy Budd* lies mainly in the status accorded to the fatal blow. If Billy represents pure goodness, then his act is unintentional but symbolically righteous, since it results in the destruction of the "evil" Claggart. If Billy is a case of neurotic repression, then his act is determined by his unconscious desires, and reveals the destructiveness of the attempt to repress one's own destructiveness. In the first case, the murder is accidental; in the second, it is the fulfillment of a wish. Strangely enough, this question of accident versus motivation is brought up again at the end of the story, in the curious lack of spontaneous ejaculation in Billy's corpse. Whether the lack of spasm is as mechanical as its presence would have been, or whether it results from what the purser calls "will power" or "euthanasia," the incident stands as a negative analogue of the murder scene. In the former, it is the absence; in the later, the presence, of physical violence that offers a challenge to interpretation. The burlesque discussion of the "prodigy of repose" by the purser and the surgeon, interrupting as it does the solemnity of Billy's "ascension," can have no other purpose than to dramatize the central importance for the story of the question of arbitrary accident versus determinable motivation. If the psychoanalytical and the metaphysical readings, however incompatible, are both equally supported by textual evidence, then perhaps Melville, rather than asking us to choose between them, is presenting us with a context in which to examine what is at stake in the very oppositions between psychoanalysis and metaphysics, chance and determination, the willed and the accidental, the unconscious and the moral.

The Deadly Space Between

> And thus do we of wisdom and of reach,
> With windlasses and with assays of bias,
> By indirections find directions out.
>
> *—Hamlet* 2.1

While Billy stands as a performative riddle (are his actions motivated or accidental?), John Claggart is presented as an enigma for cognition, a man "who for reasons of his own was keeping *incog*" (p. 343). Repeatedly referred to as a "mystery," Claggart, it seems, is difficult, even perilous, to describe:

> For the adequate comprehending of Claggart by a normal nature these hints are insufficient. To pass from a normal nature to him one must cross "the deadly space between." And this is best done by indirection. (P. 352)

Between Claggart and a "normal nature" there exists a gaping cognitive chasm. In a literal sense, this image of crossing a "deadly space" in order to reach Claggart can almost be seen as an ironic prefiguration of the murder. Billy does indeed "cross" the "space" between himself and Claggart by means of a "deadly" blow. The phrase "space between" recurs, in fact, just after the murder, to refer to the physical separation between the dead Claggart and the condemned Billy:

> Aft, and on either side, was a small stateroom, the one now temporarily a jail and the other a dead-house, and a yet smaller compartment, leaving a *space between* expanding forward. (P. 382)

It is by means of a deadly chiasmus that the spatial chasm is crossed.

But physical separation is obviously not the only kind of "deadly space" involved here. The expression "deadly space between" refers primarily to a gap in cognition, a boundary beyond which ordinary understanding does not normally go. This sort of space, which stands as a limit to comprehension, seems to be an inherent feature of the attempt to describe John Claggart. From the very beginning, Melville admits:

> His portrait I essay, but shall never hit it. (P. 342)

What Melville says he will *not* do here is precisely what Billy Budd *does* do: hit John Claggart. It would seem that speaking and killing are thus mutually exclusive; Billy Budd kills because he cannot speak, while Melville, through the very act of speaking, does not kill. Billy's fist crosses the "deadly space" directly; Melville's crossing, "done by indirection," leaves its target intact.

This state of affairs, reassuring as it sounds on a moral level, is rather unsettling, however, if one examines what it implies about Melville's writing. For how reliable can a description be if it does not hit its object? What do we come to know of John Claggart if what we learn is that his portrait is askew? If to describe perfectly, to refer adequately, would be to "hit" the referent and thus annihilate it; if to know completely would be to obliterate the very object known; if the perfect fulfillment of the constative, referential function of language would consist in the total obliteration of the object of that function; then language can retain its "innocence" only by giving up its referential validity. Melville can avoid murder only by grounding his discourse in ineradicable error. If to cross a space by indirection—that is, by rhetorical displacement—is to escape deadliness, that crossing can succeed only on the condition of radically losing its way.

It can thus be said that the "deadly space" that runs through *Billy Budd* is located between cognition and performance, knowing and doing, error and murder. But even this formulation is insufficient if it is

taken to imply that doing is deadly while speaking is not, or that directness is murderous while avoidance is innocent. Melville does not simply
recommend the replacement of doing by speaking or of direct by in-
direct language. He continues to treat obliquity and deviation as evils,
and speaks of digression as a "literary sin":

> In this matter of writing, resolve as one may to keep to the main road, some
> bypaths have an enticement not readily to be withstood. I am going to err into
> such a bypath. If the reader will keep me company I shall be glad. At the least,
> we can promise ourselves that pleasure which is wickedly said to be in sinning,
> for a literary sin the divergence will be. (p. 334)

Directness and indirectness are equally suspect and equally innocent.
Further complications of the moral status of rhetoric will be examined
later in this chapter, but first let us pursue the notion of the "deadly
space."

If the space at work in *Billy Budd* cannot be located simply and unequivocally between language and action or between directness and indirection, where is it located and how does it function? Why is it the
space itself that is called "deadly"? And how, more particularly, does
Melville go about *not* hitting John Claggart?

Melville takes up the question of Claggart's "nature" many times.
Each time, the description is proffered as a necessary key to the understanding of the story. And yet, each time, what we learn about the
master-at-arms is that we cannot learn anything:

> Nothing was known of his former life. (P. 343)

> About as much was really known to the *Bellipotent's* tars of the master-at-
> arms' career before entering the service as an astronomer knows about a
> comet's travels prior to its first observable appearance in the sky. (P. 345)

> What can more partake of the mysterious than an antipathy spontaneous and
> profound . . . ? (P. 351)

> Dark sayings are these, some will say. But why? Is it because they somewhat
> savor of Holy Writ in its phrase "mystery of iniquity?" (P. 354)

And, after informing us that the crossing of the "deadly space" between Claggart and a "normal nature" is "best done by indirection,"
Melville's narrator takes himself at his word; he digresses into a long
fictitious dialogue between himself as a youth and an older "honest
scholar" concerning a mysterious Mr. "X—" whose "labyrinth" cannot
be penetrated by "knowledge of the world," a dialogue so full of periphrases that the youthful participant himself "did not quite see" its
"drift" (p. 353). The very phrase "the deadly space between" is, according to editors Hayford and Sealts, a quotation of unknown origin;

the source of the expression used to designate what is not known is thus itself unknown. Even the seemingly satisfactory Platonic definition of Claggart's evil—"Natural Depravity: a depravity according to nature" —is in fact, as F. B. Freeman points out, nothing but a tautology. Syntactically, the definition fulfills its function, but it is empty of any cognitive information. The place of explanation and definition is repeatedly filled, but its content is always lacking. The progress of Melville's description describes an infinite regress of knowledge. The "deadly space" is situated not between Claggart and his fellow men, but within Melville's very attempts to account for him.

It would seem that rather than simply separating language from action, the space in question is also at work within language itself. In the tautology of Claggart's evil, it marks an empty articulation between the expression and its definition. Other linguistic spaces abound. What, indeed, is Billy's fateful stutter, if not a deadly gap in his ability to speak? The space opened up by the stutter is the pivot on which the entire story turns. And the last words of the dying Captain Vere, which stand in the place of ultimate commentary upon the drama, are simply "Billy Budd, Billy Budd," the empty repetition of a name. At all the crucial moments in the drama—in the origin of evil, in the trigger of the act, in the final assessment—the language of *Billy Budd* stutters. At those moments, the constative or referential content is eclipsed; language conveys only its own empty, mechanical functioning. But these very gaps in understanding are what Melville is asking us to understand.

The cognitive spaces marked out by these eclipses of meaning are important not because they mark the limits of interpretation but because they function as its cause. The gaps in understanding are never directly perceived as such by the characters in the novel; those gaps are themselves taken as interpretable signs and triggers for interpretation. The lack of knowledge of Claggart's past, for example, is seen as a sign that he has something to hide:

> Nothing was known of his former life. . . . Among certain grizzled sea gossips of the gun decks and forecastle went a rumor perdue that the master-at-arms was a *chevalier* [emphasis in original] who had volunteered into the King's navy by way of compounding for some mysterious swindle whereof he had been arraigned at the King's Bench. *The fact that nobody could substantiate this report was, of course, nothing against its secret currency.* . . . Indeed a man of Claggart's accomplishments, without prior nautical experience entering the navy at mature life, as he did, and necessarily allotted at the start to the lowest grade in it; a man too who never made allusion to his previous life ashore; these were circumstances which *in the dearth of exact knowledge* as to his true antecedents opened to the invidious *a vague field for unfavorable surmise.* (P. 343)

In other words, the absence of knowledge here leads to the propagation of tales. The absence of knowledge of Claggart's origins is not a simple, contingent, theoretically remediable lack of information; it is the very *origin* of his "evil nature." Interestingly, in Billy's case, an equal lack of knowledge leads some readers to see his origin as divine. Asked who his father is, Billy replies, "God knows." The divine and the satanic can thus be seen as metaphysical interpretations of discontinuities in knowledge. In *Billy Budd,* a stutter and a tautology serve to mark the spot from which evil springs.

Evil, then, is essentially the misreading of discontinuity through the attribution of meaning to a space or division in language. But the fact that stories of Claggart's evil arise out of a seemingly meaningless gap in knowledge is hardly a meaningless or innocent fact in itself, either in its cause or in its consequences. Claggart's function is that of a policeman "charged among other matters with the duty of preserving order on the populous lower gun decks" (p. 342). As Melville points out, "no man holding his office in a man-of-war can ever hope to be popular with the crew" (p. 345). The inevitable climate of resentment surrounding the master-at-arms might itself be sufficient to turn the hypothesis of depravity into a self-fulfilling prophecy. As Melville puts it, "The point of the present story *turn[s] on the hidden nature* of the master-at-arms" (p. 354). The entire plot of *Billy Budd* could conceivably be seen as a consequence not of what Claggart does but of what he does not say.

It is thus by means of the misreading of gaps in knowledge and of discontinuities in action that the plot of *Billy Budd* takes shape. But because Melville describes both the spaces and the readings they engender, his concentration on the vagaries of interpretive error open up within the text the possibility of substantiating quite a number of "inside narratives" different from the one with which we are explicitly presented. What Melville's tale tells is the snowballing of tale-telling. It is possible, indeed, to retell the story from a point of view that fully justifies Claggart's suspicions, merely by putting together a series of indications already available in the narrative.

1. As Billy is being taken from the merchant ship to the warship, he shouts in farewell, "And good-bye to you too, old *Rights-of-Man*" (emphasis in original). Ratcliffe, who later recounts the incident to Claggart (as is shown by the latter's referring to it in making his accusation to Vere), interprets this as "a sly slur at impressment in general, and that of himself in especial" (p. 327). The first information Claggart is likely to have gleaned on Billy Budd has thus passed through the filter of the

lieutenant's interpretation that the handsome recruit's apparent gaiety conceals resentment.

2. When Billy resolves, after seeing the flogging of another novice, "never to merit reproof," his "punctiliousness in duty" (p. 346) is laughed at by his topmates. Billy tries desperately to make his actions coincide with his desire for perfect irreproachability, but he nevertheless finds himself "getting into petty trouble" (p. 346). Billy's "unconcealed anxiety" is considered "comical" by his fellows (p. 347). It is thus Billy's obsessive concern with his own perfection that starts a second snowball rolling, since Claggart undertakes a subtle campaign of petty persecutions "to try the temper of the man" (p. 358). The instrument used by Claggart to set "little traps for the worriment of the foretopman" is a corporal called "Squeak," who, "having naturally enough concluded that his master could have no love for the sailor, made it his business, faithful understrapper that he was, to foment the ill blood by perverting to his chief certain innocent frolics of the good-natured foretopman, besides inventing for his mouth sundry contumelious epithets he claimed to have overheard him let fall" (p. 357). Again, Claggart perceives Billy only through the distortion of an unfavorable interpretation.

3. With this impression of Billy already in his mind, Claggart proceeds to take Billy's spilling of the soup across his path "not for the mere accident it assuredly was, but for the sly escape of a spontaneous feeling on Billy's part more or less answering to the antipathy on his own" (p. 356). If this is an overreading, it is important to note that the critical tendency to see sexual or religious symbolism in the soup scene operates on exactly the same assumption as that made by Claggart— what appears to be an accident is actually motivated and meaningful. Claggart's spontaneous interpretation, hidden behind his playful words ("Handsomely done"), is not only legitimate enough on its own terms, but receives unexpected confirmation in Billy's naive outburst: "There now, who says that Jemmy Legs is down on me?" This evidence of a preexisting context in which Claggart, referred to by his disrespectful nickname, has been discussed by Billy with others—apparently a number of others, although in fact it is only one person—provides all the support Claggart needs to substantiate his suspicions. And still, he is willing to try another test.

4. Claggart sends an afterguardsman to Billy at night with a proposition to join a mutinous conspiracy of impressed men. Although Billy rejects the invitation, he does not report it as loyalty demands. He is thus protecting the conspirators. Claggart's last test has been completed; Billy is a danger to the ship. In his function as chief of police, it is Claggart's duty to report the danger.

This "reversed" reading is no more—but certainly no less—legitimate than the ordinary "good versus evil" interpretation. But its very possibility—evoked not only by these behind-the-scenes hints and nuances but also by the "garbled" newspaper report—can be taken as a sign of the centrality of the question of reading posed not only *by* but also *in* the text of *Billy Budd*. Far from recounting an unequivocal "clash of opposites"[19] the confrontation between Billy and Claggart is built by a series of minute gradations and subtle insinuations. The opposites that clash here are not two *characters* but two *readings*.

Three Readings of Reading

It is no doubt significant that the character around whom the greatest critical dissent has revolved is neither the good one nor the evil one but the one who is explicitly presented as a *reader,* Captain Vere. On some level, readers of *Billy Budd* have always testified to the fact that reading, as much as killing, is at the heart of Melville's story. But how is the act of reading being manifested? And what, precisely, are its relations with the deadliness of the spaces it attempts to comprehend?

As we have noted, critical readings of *Billy Budd* have generally divided themselves into two opposing groups, the "testament of acceptance" school on the one hand and the "testament of resistance" or "irony" school on the other. The first is characterized by its tendency to take at face value the narrator's professed admiration of Vere's sagacity and the final benediction of Vere uttered by Billy. The second group is characterized by its tendency to distance the reader's point of view from that of any of the characters, including the narrator, so that the injustice of Billy's execution becomes perceptible through a process of reversal of certain explicit pronouncements within the tale. This opposition between "acceptance" and "irony" quite strikingly mirrors, as we mentioned earlier, the opposition within the story between Billy's naiveté and Claggart's paranoia. We will therefore begin our analysis of Melville's study of the nature of reading with an examination of the way in which the act of reading is manifested in the confrontation between these two characters.

It seems evident that Billy's reading method consists of taking everything at face value, while Claggart's consists of seeing a mantrap under every daisy. Yet in practice, neither of these methods is rigorously upheld. The naive reader is not naive enough to forget to edit out information too troubling to report. The instability of the space between sign and referent, normally denied by the naive reader, is called upon as an instrument whenever that same instability threatens to disturb the content of meaning itself. Billy takes every sign as transparently readable as long as what he reads is consistent with transparent peace, order, and authority. When this is not so, his reading clouds accordingly. And Claggart, for whom every sign can be read as its opposite, neglects to doubt the transparency of any sign that tends to confirm his own doubts: "the master-at-arms *never suspected the veracity*" (p. 357) of Squeak's reports. The naive believer thus refuses to believe any evidence that subverts the transparency of his beliefs, while the ironic doubter forgets to suspect the reliability of anything confirming his own suspicions.

Naiveté and irony thus stand as symmetrical opposites blinded by their very incapacity to see anything but symmetry. Claggart, in his antipathy, "can really form no conception of an *unreciprocated* malice" (p. 358). And Billy, conscious of his own blamelessness, can see nothing but pleasantness in Claggart's pleasant words: "Had the foretopman been conscious of having done or said anything to provoke the ill-will of the official, it would have been different with him, and his sight might have been purged if not sharpened. As it was, innocence was his blinder" (p. 366). Each character sees the other only through the mirror of his own reflection. Claggart, looking at Billy, mistakes his own twisted face for the face of an enemy, while Billy, recognizing in Claggart the negativity he smothers in himself, strikes out.

The naive and the ironic readers are thus equally destructive, both of themselves and of each other. It is significant that both Billy and Claggart should die. Both readings do violence to the plays of ambiguity and belief by forcing upon the text the applicability of a universal and absolute law. The one, obsessively intent on preserving peace and eliminating equivocation, murders the text; the other, seeing nothing but universal war, becomes the spot on which aberrant premonitions of negativity become truth.

But what of the third reader in the drama, Captain Vere? What can be said of a reading whose task is precisely to read the *relation* between naiveté and paranoia, acceptance and irony, murder and error?

For many readers, the function of Captain Vere has been to provide "complexity" and "reality" in an otherwise "oversimplified" allegorical confrontation:

> Billy and Claggart, who represent almost pure good and pure evil, are too simple and too extreme to satisfy the demands of realism; for character demands admixture. Their all but allegorical blackness and whiteness, however, are functional in the service of Vere's problem, and Vere, goodness knows, is real enough.[20]

Billy Budd seems different from much of the later work, less "mysterious," even didactic. . . . Its issues seem somewhat simplified, and, though the opposition of Christly Billy and Satanic Claggart is surely diagrammatic, it appears almost melodramatic in its reduction of values. Only Captain Vere seems to give the story complexity, his deliberations acting like a balance wheel in a watch, preventing a rapid, obvious resolution of the action. . . . It is Vere's decision, and the debatable rationale for it, which introduces the complexity of intimation, the ambiguity.[21]

As the locus of complexity, Captain Vere then becomes the "balance wheel" not only in the clash between good and evil but also in the clash between "accepting" and "ironic" interpretations of the story. Critical opinion has pronounced the captain "vicious" and "virtuous," "self-mythifying" and "self-sacrificing," "capable" and "cowardly," "responsible" and "criminal," "moral" and "perverted," "intellectual" and "stupid," "moderate" and "authoritarian."[22] But how does the same character provoke such diametrically opposed responses? Why is it the judge that is so passionately judged?

In order to analyze what is at stake in Melville's portrait of Vere, let us first examine the ways in which Vere's reading differs from those of Billy Budd and John Claggart:

1. While the naive/ironic dichotomy was based on a symmetry between *individuals,* Captain Vere's reading takes place within a social *structure:* the rigidly hierarchical structure of a British warship. While the naive reader (Billy) destroys the other in order to defend the self, and while the ironic reader (Claggart) destroys the self by projecting agression onto the other, the third reader (Vere) subordinates both self and other, and ultimately sacrifices both self and other, for the preservation of a political order.

2. The apparent purpose of both Billy's and Claggart's readings was to determine character; to preserve innocence or to prove guilt. Vere, on the other hand, subordinates character to action, being to doing. "A martial court," he tells his officers, "must needs in the present case confine its attention to the *blow's consequence,* which consequence justly is to be deemed not otherwise than as the *striker's deed"* (p. 384).

3. In the opposition between the metaphysical and psychoanalytical readings of Billy's deed, the deciding question was whether the blow should be considered accidental or (unconsciously) motivated. But in Vere's courtroom reading, both these alternatives are irrelevant: "Budd's intent or non-intent is nothing to the purpose" (p. 389). What matters is not the cause but the consequences of the blow.

4. The naive or literal reader takes language at face value and treats signs as *motivated;* the ironic reader assumes that the relation between

sign and meaning can be *arbitrary* and that appearances are made to be reversed. For Vere, the functions and meanings of signs are neither transparent nor reversible but fixed by socially determined *convention*. Vere's very character is determined not by a relation between his outward appearance and his inner being but by the "buttons" that signify his position in society. While both Billy and Claggart are said to owe their character to "nature," Vere sees his actions and being as meaningful only within the context of a contractual allegiance:

> Do these buttons that we wear attest that our allegiance is to Nature? No, to the King. Though the ocean, which is inviolate Nature primeval, though this be the element where we move and have our being as sailors, yet as the King's officers lies our duty in a sphere correspondingly natural? So little is that true, that in receiving our commissions we in the most important regards ceased to be natural free agents. When war is declared are we the commissioned fighters previously consulted? We fight at command. If our judgments approve the war, that is but coincidence. (P. 387)

Judgment is thus for Vere a function neither of individual conscience nor of absolute justice but of "the rigor of martial law" (p. 387) operating *through* him.

5. While Billy and Claggart read spontaneously and directly, Vere's reading often makes use of precedent (historical facts, childhood memories), allusions (to the Bible, to various ancient and modern authors), and analogies (Billy is like Adam, Claggart is like Ananias). Just as both Billy and Claggart have no known past, they read without memory; just as their lives end with their reading, they read without foresight. Vere, on the other hand, interrogates both past and future for interpretative guidance.

6. While Budd and Claggart thus oppose each other directly, without regard for circumstance or consequence, Vere reads solely in function of the attending historical situation; the Nore and Spithead mutinies have created an atmosphere "critical to naval authority" (p. 380), and, since an engagement with the enemy fleet is possible at any moment, the *Bellipotent* cannot afford internal unrest.

The fundamental factor that underlies the opposition between the metaphysical Budd/Claggart conflict on the one hand and the reading of Captain Vere on the other can be summed up in a single word: history. While the naive and the ironic readers attempt to impose upon language the functioning of an absolute, timeless, universal law (the sign as either motivated or arbitrary), the question of *martial* law arises within the story precisely to reveal the law as a historical phenomenon, to underscore the element of contextual mutability in the conditions of any act of reading. Arbitrariness and motivation, irony and literality, are parameters between which language constantly fluctuates, but only historical context determines which proportion of each is perceptible to each reader. Melville indeed shows history to be a story not only of events but also of fluctuations in the very functioning of irony and belief:

> The event *converted into irony for a time* those spirited strains of Dibdin. . . . (P. 333)

> Everything is *for a term venerated* in navies. (P. 408)

The opposing critical judgments of Vere's decision to hang Billy are divided, in the final analysis, according to the place they attribute to history in the process of justification. For the ironists, Vere is misusing history for his own self-preservation or for the preservation of a world safe for aristocracy. For those who accept Vere's verdict as tragic but necessary, it is Melville who has stacked the historical cards in Vere's favor. In both cases, the conception of history as an interpretive instrument remains the same: it is its *use* that is being judged. And the very direction of *Billy Budd* criticism itself, historically moving from acceptance to irony, is no doubt itself interpretable in the same historical terms.

Evidence can be found in the text for both pro-Vere and anti-Vere judgments:

> Full of disquietude and misgiving, the surgeon left the cabin. Was Captain Vere suddenly affected in his mind? (P. 378)

> Whether Captain Vere, as the surgeon professionally and privately surmised, was really the sudden victim of any degree of aberration, every one must determine for himself by such light as this narrative may afford. (P. 379–80)

> That the unhappy event which has been narrated could not have happened at a worse juncture was but too true. For it was close on the heel of the suppressed insurrections, an aftertime very critical to naval authority, demanding from every English sea commander two qualities not readily interfusable—prudence and rigor. (P. 380)

> Small wonder then that the *Bellipotent*'s captain . . . felt that circumspection not less than promptitude was necessary. . . . Here he may or may not have erred. (P. 380)

The effect of these explicit oscillations of judgment within the text is to underline the importance of the act of judging while rendering its outcome undecidable. Judgment, however difficult, is clearly the central preoccupation of Melville's text, whether it be the judgment pronounced *by* Vere or *upon* him.

There is still another reason for the uncertainty over Vere's final status, however: the unfinished state of the manuscript at Melville's death. According to editors Hayford and Sealts,[23] it is the "late pencil revisions" that cast the greatest doubt upon Vere; Melville was evidently still fine-tuning the text's attitude toward its third reader when he died. The ultimate irony in the tale is thus that our final judgment of the very reader who takes history into consideration is made problematic by the intervention of history; by the historical accident of the author's death. History here affects interpretation not only within the content of the narration but also within the very production of the narrative. And what remains suspended by this historical accident is nothing less than the exact signifying value of history. Clearly, the meaning of "history" as a feature distinguishing Vere's reading from those of Claggart and Budd can in no way be taken for granted.

Judgment as Political Performance

> When a poet takes his seat on the tripod of the Muse, he cannot control his thoughts. . . . When he represents men with contrasting characters he is often obliged to contradict himself, and he doesn't know which of the opposing speeches contains the truth. But for the legislator, this is impossible: he must not let his laws say two different things on the same subject.
>
> —Plato, *The Laws*

In the final analysis, the question is not, What did Melville really think of Captain Vere? but rather, What is at stake in his way of presenting him? What can we learn from him about the act of judging? Melville seems to be presenting us less with an object for judgment than with an example of judgment. And the very vehemence with which the critics tend to praise or condemn the justice of Vere's decision indicates that it is judging, not murdering, that Melville is asking us to judge.

And yet Vere's judgment *is* an act of murder. Captain Vere is a reader who kills, not, like Billy, instead of speaking, but rather, precisely by means of speaking. While Billy kills through verbal impotence, Vere kills through the very potency and sophistication of rhetoric. Judging, in Vere's case, is nothing less than the wielding of the power of life and death through language. In thus occupying the point at which murder and language meet, Captain Vere positions himself astride the "deadly space between." While Billy's performative force occupies the vanishing point of utterance and cognition, and while the validity of Claggart's cognitive perception is realized only through the annihilation of the perceiver, Captain Vere's reading mobilizes both power and knowledge, performance and cognition, error and murder. Judgment is cognition functioning as an act. This combination of performance and cognition defines Vere's reading not merely as historical but as political. If politics is defined as the attempt to reconcile action with understanding, then Melville's story offers an exemplary context in which to analyze the interpretive and performative structures that make politics so problematic.

Melville's story amply demonstrates that the alliance between knowledge and action is by no means an easy one. Vere indeed has often been seen as the character in the tale who experiences the greatest suffering; his understanding of Billy's character and his military duty are totally at odds. On the one hand, cognitive exactitude requires that "history" be taken into consideration. Yet what constitutes "knowledge of history"? How are "circumstances" to be defined? What sort of causality does "precedent" imply? And what is to be done with overlapping but incompatible "contexts"? Before deciding upon innocence and guilt, Vere must define and limit the frame of reference within which his decision is to be possible. He does so by choosing the "legal" context over the "essential" context:

> In a *legal view* the apparent victim of the tragedy was he who had sought to victimize a man blameless; and the indisputable deed of the latter, *navally regarded*, constituted the most heinous of military crimes. Yet more. The *essential right and wrong* involved in the matter, the clearer that might be, so much the worse for the responsibility of a loyal sea commander, inasmuch as he was not authorized to determine the matter on that primitive basis. (P. 380)

Yet it is precisely this determination of the proper frame of reference that dictates the outcome of the decision; once Vere has defined his context, he has also in fact reached his verdict. The very choice of the *conditions* of judgment itself constitutes a judgment. But what are the conditions of choosing the conditions of judgment?

The alternative, it seems, is between the "naval" and the "primitive," between "Nature" and "the King," between the martial court and what Vere calls the "Last Assizes" (p. 388). But the question arises of exactly what the concept "Nature" entails in such an opposition. In what way, and with what changes, would it have been possible for Vere's allegiance to be to "Nature"? How can a legal judgment exemplify "primitive" justice?

In spite of his allegiance to martial law and conventional authority, Vere clearly finds the "absolute" criteria equally applicable to Billy's deed, for he responds to each new development with the following exclamations:

> "It is the divine judgment on Ananias!" (P. 278)

> "Struck dead by an angel of God! Yet the angel must hang!" (P. 378)
>
> "Before a court less arbitrary and more merciful than a martial one, that plea would largely extenuate. At the Last Assizes it shall acquit." (P. 388)
>
> "Ay, there is a mystery; but, to use a scriptural phrase, it is a 'mystery of iniquity,' a matter for psychologic theologicans to discuss." (P. 385)

This last expression, which refers to the source of Claggart's antipathy, has already been mentioned by Melville's narrator and dismissed as being "tinctured with the biblical element":

> If that lexicon which is based on Holy Writ were any longer popular, one might with less difficulty define and denominate certain phenomenal men. As it is, one must turn to some authority not liable to the charge of being tinctured with the biblical element. (P. 353)

Vere turns to the Bible to designate Claggart's "nature"; Melville turns to a Platonic tautology. But in both cases, the question arises, What does it mean to seal an explanation with a quotation? And what, in Vere's case, does it mean to refer a legal mystery to a religious text?

If Vere names the "absolute"—as opposed to the martial—by means of quotations and allusions, does this not suggest that the two alternative frames of reference within which judgment is possible are not nature and the king, but rather two types of textual authority: the Bible and the Mutiny Act? This is not to say that Vere is "innocently" choosing one text over another, but that the nature of "nature" in a legal context cannot be taken for granted. Even Thomas Paine, who is referred to by Melville in his function as proponent of "natural" human rights, cannot avoid grounding his concept of nature in biblical myth. In the very act of rejecting the authority of antiquity, he writes:

> The fact is, that portions of antiquity, by proving every thing, establish nothing. It is authority against authority all the way, till we come to the divine origin of the rights of man, at the Creation. Here our inquiries find a resting-place, and our reason finds a home.[24]

The final frame of reference is neither the heart nor the gun, neither nature nor the king, but the authority of a sacred text. Authority seems to be nothing other than the vanishing-point of textuality. And nature is authority whose textual origins have been forgotten. Even behind the martial order of the world of the man-of-war, there lies a religious referent: the *Bellipotent*'s last battle is with a French ship called the *Athée*.

Judgment, then, would seem to ground itself in a suspension of the opposition between textuality and referentiality, just as politics can be seen as that which makes it impossible to draw the line between "language" and "life." Vere, indeed, is presented as a reader who does not recognize the "frontier" between "remote allusions" and current events:

> In illustrating of any point touching the stirring personages and events of the time he would be as apt to cite some historic character or incident of antiquity as he would be to cite from the moderns. He seemed unmindful of the circumstances that to his bluff company such remote allusions, however pertinent they might really be, were altogether alien to men whose reading was mainly confined to the journals. But considerateness in such matters is not easy to natures constituted like Captain Vere's. Their honesty prescribes to them directness, sometimes far-reaching like that of a migratory fowl that in its flight never heeds when it crosses a frontier. (P. 341)

Yet it is by inviting Billy Budd and John Claggart to "cross" the "frontier" between their proper territory and their superior's cabin, between the private and the political realms, that Vere unwittingly sets up the conditions for the narrative chiasmus he must judge.

As was noted earlier, Captain Vere's function, according to many critics, is to insert "ambiguity" into the story's "oversimplified" allegorical opposition. Yet, at the same time, it is Captain Vere who inspires the most vehement critical oppositions. In other words, he seems to mobilize simultaneously the seemingly contradictory forces of ambiguity and polarity.

In his median position between the Budd/Claggart opposition and the acceptance/irony opposition, Captain Vere functions as a focus for the conversion of polarity into ambiguity and back again. Interestingly, he plays exactly the same role in the progress of the plot. It is Vere who brings together the "innocent" Billy and the "guilty" Claggart in order to test the validity of Claggart's accusations, but he does so in such a way as to effect not a clarification but a reversal of places between guilt and innocence. Vere's fatherly words to Billy trigger the ambiguous deed upon which Vere must pronounce a verdict of "condemn *or* let go." Just as Melville's readers, faced with the ambiguity they themselves recognize as being provided by Vere, are quick to pronounce the captain vicious *or* virtuous, evil *or* just; so, too, Vere, who clearly perceives the "mystery" in the "moral dilemma" confronting him, must nevertheless reduce the situation to a binary opposition.

It would seem, then, that the function of judgment is to convert an ambiguous situation into a decidable one. But it does so by converting a difference *within* (Billy as divided between conscious submissiveness and unconscious hostility, Vere as divided between understanding father and military authority) into a difference *between* (between Claggart and Billy, between Nature and the King, between authority and criminality). A difference *between* opposing forces presupposes that the entities in conflict be knowable. A difference *within* one of the entities in question is precisely what problematizes the very *idea* of an entity in the first place, rendering the "legal point of view" inapplicable. In studying the plays of both ambiguity and binarity, Melville's story situates *its* critical difference neither within nor between, but in the *relation between the two* as the fundamental question of all human politics. The political context in *Billy Budd* is such that on all levels the differences *within* (mutiny on the warship, the French revolution as a threat to "lasting institutions," Billy's unconscious hostility) are subordinated to differences *between* (the *Bellipotent* vs. the *Athée*, England vs. France, murderer vs. victim). This is why Melville's choice of historical setting is so significant; the war between France and England at the time of the French Revolution is as striking an example of the simultaneous functioning of differences within and between as is the confrontation between Billy and Claggart in relation to their own internal divisions. War, indeed, is the absolute transformation of all differences into binary differences.

It would seem, then, that the maintenance of political authority requires that the law function as a set of rules for the regular, predictable misreading of the "difference within" as a "difference between." Yet if, as our epigraph from Plato suggests, law is thus defined in terms of its repression of ambiguity, then it is itself an overwhelming example of an entity based on a "difference within." Like Billy, the law, in attempting to eliminate its own "deadly space," can only inscribe itself in a space of deadliness.

In seeking to regulate the violent effects of difference, the political work of cognition is thus an attempt to situate that which must be eliminated. Yet in the absence of the possibility of knowing the locus and origin of violence, cognition itself becomes an act of violence. In terms of pure understanding, the drawing of a line between opposing entities does violence to the irreducible ambiguities that subvert the very possibility of determining the limits of what an "entity" is:

> Who in the rainbow can draw the line where the violet tint ends and the orange tint begins? Distinctly we see the difference of the colors, but where exactly does the first blendingly enter into the other? So with sanity and insanity. In pronounced cases there is no question about them. But in some supposed cases, in various degrees supposedly less pronounced, to draw the exact line of demarcation few will undertake, though for a fee becoming considerate some professional experts will. There is nothing nameable but that some men will, or undertake to, do it for pay. (P. 379)

As an act, drawing a line is inexact and violent; and it also problematizes the very possibility of situating the "difference between" the judge and what is judged, between the interests of the "expert" and the truth of his expertise. What every act of judgment manifests is not the value of the object but the position of the judge within a structure of exchange. There is, in other words, no position from which to judge that would be outside the lines of force involved in the object judged.

But if judging is always a *partial* reading (in both senses of the word), is there a place for reading beyond politics? Are we, as Melville's readers, outside the arena in which power and fees are exchanged? If law is the forcible transformation of ambiguity into decidability, is it possible to read ambiguity *as such,* without that reading functioning as a political act?

Melville has something to say even about this. For there is a fourth reader in *Billy Budd,* one who "never interferes in aught and never gives advice" (p. 363): the old Dansker. A man of "few words, many wrinkles" and "the complexion of an antique parchment" (p. 347), the Dansker is the very picture of one who understands and emits ambiguous utterances. When asked by Billy for an explanation of his petty troubles, the Dansker says only, "Jemmy Legs [Claggart] is down on you" (p. 349). This interpretation, entirely accurate as a reading of Claggart's ambiguous behavior, is handed down to Billy without further explanation:

> Something less unpleasantly oracular he tried to extract; but the old sea Chiron, thinking perhaps that for the nonce he had sufficiently instructed his young Achilles, pursed his lips, gathered all his wrinkles together, and would commit himself to nothing further. (P. 349)

As a reader who understands ambiguity yet refuses to "commit himself," the Dansker thus dramatizes a reading that attempts to be as cognitively accurate and as performatively neutral as possible. Yet however neutral he tries to remain, the Dansker's reading does not take place outside the political realm; it is his very refusal to participate in it, whether by further instruction or by direct intervention, that leads to Billy's exclamation in the soup episode ("There now, who says Jemmy Legs is down on me?"). The transference of knowledge is no more innocent than the transference of power, for it is through the impossibility of finding a spot from which knowledge could be all-encompassing that the plays of political power proceed.

Just as the attempt to know without doing can itself function as a deed, the fact that judgment is always explicitly an act adds a further insoluble problem to its cognitive predicament. Since, as Vere points out, no judgment can take place in the "*Last* Assizes," no judge can ever pronounce a Last Judgment. In order to reach a verdict, Vere must determine the consequences not only of the fatal blow but also of his own verdict. Judgment is an act not only because it kills, but because it is in turn open to judgment:

> "Can we not convict and yet mitigate the penalty?" asked the sailing master. . . .
>
> "Gentlemen, were that clearly lawful for us under the circumstances, consider the consequences of such clemency. . . . To the people the foretopman's deed, however it be worded in the announcement, will be plain homicide committed in a flagrant act of mutiny. What penalty for that should follow, they know. But it does not follow. *Why?* They will ruminate. You know what sailors are. Will they not revert to the recent outbreak at the Nore?" (P. 389)

The danger is not only one of repeating the Nore mutiny, however. It is also one of forcing Billy, for all his innocence, to repeat his crime. Billy is a politically charged object from the moment he strikes his superior. He is no longer, and can never again be, plotless. If he were set free, he himself would be unable to explain why. As a focus for the questions and intrigues of the crew, he would be even less capable of defending himself than before, and would surely strike again. The political reading, as cognition, attempts to understand the past; as performance, it attempts to eliminate from the future any necessity for its own recurrence.

What this means is that every judge is in the impossible position of having to include the effects of his own act of judging within the cognitive context of his decision. The question of the nature of the type of historical causality that would govern such effects can neither be decided nor ignored. Because of his official position, Vere cannot choose to read in such a way that his reading would not be an act of political authority. But Melville shows in *Billy Budd* that authority consists precisely in the impossibility of containing the effects of its own application.

As a political allegory, Melville's *Billy Budd* is thus much more than a study of good and evil, justice and injustice. It is a dramatization of the twisted relations between knowing and doing, speaking and killing, reading and judging, which make political understanding and action so problematic. In the subtle creation of Claggart's "evil" out of a series of spaces in knowledge, Melville shows that gaps in cognition, far from being mere absences, take on the performative power of true acts. The *force* of what is not known is all the more effective for not being perceived as such. The crew, which does not understand that it does not know, is no less performative a reader than the captain, who clearly perceives and represses the presence of "mystery." The legal order, which

attempts to submit "brute force" to "forms, measured forms," can only eliminate violence by transforming violence into the final authority.
And cognition, which perhaps begins as a power play against the play of
power, can only increase, through its own elaboration, the range of
what it tries to dominate. The "deadly space" or "difference" that runs
through *Billy Budd* is not located between knowledge and action, performance and cognition. It is that which, within cognition, functions as
an act; it is that which, within action, prevents us from ever knowing
whether what we hit coincides with what we understand. And this is
what makes the meaning of Melville's last work so *striking.*

7. The Frame of Reference: Poe, Lacan, Derrida

The Purloined Preface

A literary text that both analyzes itself and shows that it actually has neither a self nor any neutral metalanguage with which to do the analyzing, calls out irresistibly for analysis. When that call is answered by two eminent French thinkers whose readings emit their own equally paradoxical call-to-analysis, the resulting triptych, in the context of the question of the act-of-reading (-literature), places its would-be reader in a vertiginously insecure position.

The three texts in question are Edgar Allan Poe's short story "The Purloined Letter," Jacques Lacan's "Seminar on The Purloined Letter" and Jacques Derrida's reading of Lacan's reading of Poe, "The Purveyor of Truth" ("Le Facteur de la Vérité").[1] In all three texts, it is the *act of analysis* which seems to occupy the center of the discursive stage, and the *act of analysis of the act of analysis* which in some way disrupts that centrality. In the resulting asymmetrical, abyssal structure, no analysis—including this one—can intervene without transforming and repeating other elements in the sequence, which is thus not a stable sequence, but which nevertheless produces certain regular effects. It is the functioning of this regularity, and the structure of these effects, which will provide the basis for the present study.

The subversion of any possibility of a position of analytical mastery occurs in many ways. Here, the very fact that we are dealing with *three* texts is in no way certain. Poe's story not only fits into a triptych of its own, but is riddled with a constant, peculiar kind of intertextuality (the epigraph from Seneca which is not from Seneca, the lines from

Crébillon's *Atrée* which serve as Dupin's signature, etc.). Lacan's text not only presents itself backwards (its introduction *following* its conclusion), but it never finishes presenting itself (*"Ouverture de ce recueil," "Présentation de la suite," "Présentation"* to the *Points* edition). And Derrida's text is not only preceded by several years of annunciatory marginalia and footnotes but is itself structured by its own deferment, its *différance* (cf. the repetition of such expressions as "mais nous n'en sommes pas encore là" ["but we are getting ahead of ourselves"], etc.). In addition, an unusually high degree of apparent digressiveness characterizes these texts, to the point of making the reader wonder whether there is really any true subject matter there at all. It is as though any attempt to follow the path of the purloined letter is automatically purloined from itself. Which is, as we shall see, just what the letter has always already been saying.

Any attempt to do "justice" to three such complex texts is obviously out of the question. But in each of these readings of the act of analysis the very question being asked is, What is the nature of such "justice"? It can hardly be an accident that the debate proliferates around a *crime* story—a robbery and its undoing. Somewhere in each of these texts, the economy of justice cannot be avoided. For in spite of the absence of mastery, there is no lack of effects of power.

As the reader goes on with this series of prefatory remarks, he may begin to see how contagious the deferment of the subject of the purloined letter can be. But the problem of how to present these three texts is all the more redoubtable since each of them both presents itself and the others, and clearly shows the fallacies inherent in any type of "presentation" of a text. It is small comfort that such fallacies are not only inevitable but also *constitutive* of any act of reading—also demonstrated by each of the texts—since the resulting injustices, however unavoidable in general, always appear corrigible in detail. Which is why the sequence continues.

The question of how to present to the reader a text too extensive to quote in its entirety has long been one of the underlying problems of literary criticism. Since a shorter version of the text must somehow be produced, two solutions constantly recur: paraphrase and quotation. Although these tactics are seldom if ever used in isolation, the specific configuration of their combinations and permutations determines to a large extent the "plot" of the critical narrative to which they give rise. The first act of our own narrative, then, will consist of an analysis of the strategic effects of the use of paraphrase versus quotation in each of the three texts in question.

Round Robbin'

> *Round robin:* 1) A tournament in which each contestant is matched against every other contestant. 2) A petition or protest on which the signatures are arranged in the form of a circle in order to conceal the order of signing. 3) A letter sent among members of a group, often with comments added by each person in turn. 4) An extended sequence.
>
> —*American Heritage Dictionary*

In 1845, Edgar Allan Poe published the third of his three detective stories, "The Purloined Letter," in a collective volume entitled—ironically, considering all the robberies in the story—*The Gift: A Christmas, New Year, and Birthday Present.* "The Purloined Letter" is a first-person narration of two scenes in which dialogues occur among the narrator, his friend C. Auguste Dupin, and, initially, the Prefect of the Parisian police. The two scenes are separated by an indication of the passage of a month's time. In each of the two dialogues, reported to us verbatim by the narrator, one of the other two characters tells the story of a robbery. In the first scene, it is the Prefect of Police who repeats the Queen's eyewitness account of the Minister's theft of a letter addressed to her; in the second scene, it is Dupin who narrates his own theft of the same letter from the Minister, who had meanwhile readdressed it to himself. In a paragraph placed between these two "crime" stories, the narrator himself narrates a wordless scene in which the letter changes hands again before his eyes, passing from Dupin—not without the latter's having addressed not the letter but a check to himself—to the Prefect (who will pocket the remainder of the reward) and thence, presumably, back to the Queen.

By appearing to repeat to us faithfully every word in both dialogues, the narrator would seem to have resorted exclusively to direct quotation in presenting his story. Even when paraphrase could have been expected—in the description of the exact procedures employed by the police in searching unsuccessfully for the letter, for example,—we are spared none of the details. Thus it is all the more surprising to find that there *is* one little point at which direct quotation of the Prefect's words gives way to paraphrase. This point, however brief, is of no small importance, as we shall see. It occurs in the concluding paragraph of the first scene:

> "I have no better advice to give you," said Dupin. "You have, of course, an accurate description of the letter?"
> "Oh, yes!"—And here the Prefect, producing a memorandum-book, proceeded to read aloud a minute account of the internal, and especially of the external, appearance of the missing document. Soon after finishing the perusal

of this description, he took his departure, more entirely depressed in spirits than I had ever known the good gentleman before. (Poe, Pp. 206-7)

What is paraphrased is thus the description of the letter the story is about. And, whereas it is generally supposed that the function of paraphrase is to strip off the form of a speech in order to give us only its contents, here the use of paraphrase does the very opposite: it withholds the contents of the Prefect's remarks, giving us only their form. And what is swallowed up in this ellipsis is nothing less than the contents of the letter itself. The fact that the letter's message is never revealed, which will serve as the basis for Lacan's reading of the story, is thus negatively made explicit by the functioning of Poe's text itself, through what Derrida might have called a repression of the written word (a suppression of what is written in the memorandum-book—and in the letter). And the question of the strategic use of paraphrase versus quotation begins to invade the literary text as well as the critical narrative.

Lacan's presentation of Poe's text involves the paraphrase, or plot summary, of the two thefts as they are told to the narrator by the Prefect and by Dupin. Since Derrida, in his critique of Lacan, chooses to quote Lacan's paraphrase, we can combine all the tactics involved by, in our turn, quoting Derrida's quotation of Lacan's paraphrase of Poe's quoted narrations.[2]

> There are two scenes, the first of which we shall straightway designate the primal scene, and by no means inadvertently, since the second may be considered its repetition in the very sense we are considering today.
>
> The primal scene is thus performed, we are told [by neither Poe, nor the scriptor, nor the narrator, but by G, the Prefect of Police who is *mis en scène* by all those involved in the dialogues—J.D.[3]] in the royal *boudoir*, so that we suspect that the person of the highest rank, called the "exalted personage," who is alone there when she receives a letter, is the Queen. This feeling is confirmed by the embarrassment into which she is plunged by the entry of the other exalted personage, of whom we have already been told [again by G—J.D.] prior to this account that the knowledge he might have of the letter in question would jeopardize for the lady nothing less than her honor and safety. Any doubt that he is in fact the King is promptly dissipated in the course of the scene which begins with the entry of Minister D. . . . At that moment, in fact, the Queen can do no better than to play on the King's inattentiveness by leaving the letter on the table "face down, address uppermost." It does not, however, escape the Minister's lynx eye, nor does he fail to notice the Queen's distress and thus to fathom her secret. From then on everything transpires like clockwork. After dealing in his customary manner with the business of the day, the Minister draws from his pocket a letter similar in appearance to the one in his view, and having pretended to read it, places it next to the other. A bit more conversation to amuse the royal company, whereupon,

without flinching once, he seizes the embarrassing letter, making off with it, as the Queen, on whom none of his maneuver has been lost, remains unable to intervene for fear of attracting the attention of her royal spouse, close at her side at that very moment.

Everything might then have transpired unseen by a hypothetical spectator of an operation in which nobody falters, and whose *quotient* is that the Minister has filched from the Queen her letter and that—an even more important result than the first—the Queen knows that he now has it, and by no means innocently.

A *remainder* that no analyst will neglect, trained as he is to retain whatever is significant, without always knowing what to do with it: the letter, abandoned by the Minister, and which the Queen's hand is now free to roll into a ball.

Second scene: in the Minister's office. It is in his hotel, and we know—from the account the Prefect of Police has given Dupin, whose specific genius for solving enigmas Poe introduces here for the second time—that the police, returning there as soon as the Minister's habitual nightly absences allow them to, have searched the hotel and its surroundings from top to bottom for the last eighteen months. In vain,—although everyone can deduce from the situation that the Minister keeps the letter within reach.

Dupin calls on the Minister. The latter receives him with studied nonchalance, affecting in his conversation romantic *ennui*. Meanwhile Dupin, whom this pretence does not deceive, his eyes protected by green glasses, proceeds to inspect the premises. When his glance catches a rather crumbled piece of paper —apparently thrust carelessly in a division of an ugly pasteboard card-rack, hanging gaudily from the middle of the mantelpiece—he already knows that he's found what he's looking for. His conviction is reinforced by the very details which seem to contradict the description he has of the stolen letter, with the exception of the format, which remains the same.

Whereupon he has but to withdraw, after "forgetting" his snuff-box on the table, in order to return the following day to reclaim it—armed with a facsimile of the letter in its present state. As an incident in the street, prepared for the proper moment, draws the Minister to the window, Dupin in turn seizes the opportunity to seize the letter while substituting the imitation, and has only to maintain the appearances of a normal exit.

Here as well all has transpired, if not without noise, at least without all commotion. The quotient of the operation is that the Minister no longer has the letter, but, far from suspecting that Dupin is the culprit who has ravished it from him, knows nothing of it. Moreover, what he is left with is far from insignificant for what follows. We shall return to what brought Dupin to inscribe a message on his counterfeit letter. Whatever the case, the Minister, when he tries to make use of it, will be able to read these words, written so that he may recognize Dupin's hand: ". . . Un dessein si funeste / S'il n'est digne d'Atrée est digne de Thyeste,"[4] whose source, Dupin tells us, is Crébillon's *Atrée*.

Need we emphasize the similarity of these two sequences? Yes, for the resemblance we have in mind is not a simple collection of traits chosen only in order to delete their difference. And it would not be enough to retain those common traits at the expense of the others for the slightest truth to result. It is rather the intersubjectivity in which the two actions are motivated that we wish to bring into relief, as well as the three terms through which it structures them.

The special status of these terms results from their corresponding simultaneously to the three logical moments through which the decision is precipitated and the three places it assigns to the subjects among whom it constitutes a choice.

That decision is reached in a glance's time. For the maneuvers which follow, however stealthily they prolong it, add nothing to that glance, nor does the deferring of the deed in the second scene break the unity of that moment.

This glance presupposes two others, which it embraces in its vision of the breach left in their fallacious complementarity, anticipating in it the occasion for larceny afforded by that exposure. Thus three moments, structuring three glances, borne by three subjects, incarnated each time by different characters.

The first is a glance that sees nothing: the King and the police.

The second, a glance which sees that the first sees nothing and deludes itself as to the secrecy of what it hides: the Queen, then the Minister.

The third sees that the first two glances leave what should be hidden exposed to whoever would seize it: the Minister and finally Dupin.

In order to grasp in its unity the intersubjective complex thus described, we would willingly seek a model in the technique legendarily attributed to the ostrich attempting to shield itself from danger; for that technique might ultimately be qualified as political, divided as it here is among three partners: the second believing itself invisible because the first has its head stuck in the ground, and all the while letting the third calmly pluck its rear; we need only enrich its proverbial denomination by a letter, producing *la politique de l'autruiche,*[5] for the ostrich itself to take on forever a new meaning.

Given the intersubjective modulus of the repetitive action, it remains to recognize in it a *repetition automatism* in the sense that interests us in Freud's text. (SPL, pp. 41-44; PT, pp. 54-57)

Thus, it is neither the character of the individual subjects, nor the contents of the letter, but the position of the letter within the group which decides what each person will do next. Because the letter does not function as a unit of meaning (a *signified*) but as that which produces certain effects (a *signifier*), Lacan reads the story as an illustration of "the truth which may be drawn from that moment in Freud's thought under study—namely, that it is the symbolic order which is constitutive for the subject—by demonstrating . . . the decisive orientation which the subject receives from the itinerary of a signifier" (SPL, p. 40). The letter acts like a signifier to the extent that its function in the story does not require that its meaning be revealed: "the letter was able to produce its effects *within* the story: on the actors in the tale, including the narrator, as well as *outside* the story: on us, the readers, and also on its author, without anyone's ever bothering to worry about what it *meant*" (not translated in SPL; *Ecrits,* p. 57, translation and emphasis mine). "The Purloined Letter" thus becomes for Lacan a kind of *allegory of the signifier.*

Derrida's critique of Lacan's reading does not dispute the validity of the allegorical interpretation on its own terms, but questions its implicit presuppositions and its modus operandi. Derrida aims his objections at two kinds of target: (1) what Lacan puts into the letter and (2) what Lacan leaves out of the text.

1. *What Lacan puts into the letter.* While asserting that the letter's meaning is lacking, Lacan, according to Derrida, makes this lack into *the* meaning of the letter. But Derrida does not stop there. He goes on to assert that what Lacan means by that lack is the truth of lack-as-castration-as-truth: "The truth of the purloined letter is the truth itself. . . . What is veiled/unveiled in this case is a hole, a non-being [non-étant]; the truth of being [l'être], as non-being. Truth is 'woman' as veiled/unveiled castration" (PT, pp. 60–61). Lacan himself, however, never uses the word *castration* in the text of the original "Seminar." That it is suggested is indisputable, but Derrida, by filling in what *Lacan* left blank, is repeating the same gesture of blank-filling for which he criticizes Lacan.

2. *What Lacan leaves out of the text.* This objection is itself double: on the one hand, Derrida criticizes Lacan for neglecting to consider "The Purloined Letter" in connection with the other two stories in what Derrida calls Poe's "Dupin Trilogy." And on the other hand, according to Derrida, at the very moment Lacan is reading the story as an allegory of the signifier, he is being blind to the disseminating power of the signifier in the *text* of the allegory, in what Derrida calls the "scene of writing." To cut out part of a text's frame of reference as though it did not exist and to reduce a complex textual functioning to a single meaning are serious blots indeed in the annals of literary criticism. Therefore it is all the more noticeable that Derrida's own reading of Lacan's text repeats the crimes of which he accuses it: on the one hand, Derrida makes no mention of Lacan's long development on the relation between symbolic determination and random series. And on the other hand, Derrida dismisses Lacan's "style" as a mere ornament, veiling, for a time, an unequivocal message: "Lacan's 'style,' moreover, was such that for a long time it would hinder and delay all access to a *unique* content or a single unequivocal meaning determinable beyond the writing itself" (PT, p. 40). Derrida's repetition of the very gestures he is criticizing does not in itself invalidate his criticism of their effects, but it does problematize his statement condemning their existence.

What kind of logic is it that thus seems to turn one-upmanship into inevitable one-downmanship?

It is the very logic of the purloined letter.

Odd Couples

> Je tiens la reine!
>   O sûr châtiment . . .
>   —Mallarmé, "L'après-midi d'un faune"

> L'ascendant que le ministre tire de la situation ne tient donc pas à la lettre,
> mais, qu'il le sache ou non, au personnage qu'elle lui constitue.
>   —Lacan, SPL.

We have just seen how Derrida, in his effort to right (write) Lacan's wrongs, can, on a certain level, only repeat them, and how the rectification of a previous injustice somehow irresistibly dictates the filling in of a blank which then becomes the new injustice. In fact, the act of clinching one's triumph by filling in a blank is already prescribed in all its details within Poe's story, in Dupin's unwillingness to "leave the interior blank" (Poe, p. 219) in the facsimile he has left for the Minister, in place of the purloined letter he, Dupin, has just repossessed by means of a precise repetition of the act of robbery he is undoing. What is written in the blank is a quotation-as-signature, which curiously resembles Derrida's initialed interventions in the passages he quotes from Lacan, a resemblance on which Derrida is undoubtedly playing. And the text of the quotation transcribed by Dupin describes the structure of rectification-as-repetition-of-the-crime which has led to its being transcribed in the first place:

>   —Un dessein si funeste,
> S'il n'est digne d'Atrée, est digne de Thyeste.

Atreus, whose wife had long ago been seduced by Thyestes, is about to make Thyestes eat (literally) the fruit of that illicit union, his son Plisthenes. The avenger's plot may not be worthy of him, says Atreus, but his brother Thyestes deserves it. What the addressee of the violence is going to get is simply his own message backwards. It is this vengeful anger that, as both Lacan and Derrida show, places Dupin as one of the "ostriches" in the "triad." Not content simply to return the letter to its "rightful" destination, Dupin jumps into the fray as the wronged victim himself, by recalling an "evil turn" the minister once did him in Vienna and for which he is now, personally, taking his revenge.

Correction must thus posit a previous pretextual, pre-textual crime that will justify its excesses. Any degree of violence is permissible in the act of getting even ("To be *even* with him," says Dupin, "I complained of my weak eyes" [Poe, p. 216, emphasis mine]). And Dupin's backward revision of the story repeats itself in his readers as well. The existence of the same kind of prior aggression on Lacan's part is posited by

Derrida in a long footnote in his book *Positions,* in which he outlines what will later develop into *Le Facteur de la Vérité:* "In the texts I have published up to now, the absence of reference to Lacan is indeed almost total. That is *justified* not only by the *acts of aggression* in the form of, or with the intention of, reappropriation which, ever since *De la grammatologie* appeared in *Critique* (1965) (and even earlier, I am told) Lacan has multiplied. . ." (emphasis mine). The priority of aggression is doubled by the aggressiveness of priority: "At the time of my first publications, Lacan's *Ecrits* had not yet been collected and published. . . ."[6] And Lacan, in turn, mentions in his *Presentation* to the "Points" edition of his *Ecrits:* "what I properly call the instance of the letter *before any grammatology*"[7] (emphasis mine). The rivalry over something neither man will credit the other with possessing, the retrospective revision of the origins of both their resemblances and their differences, thus spirals backward and forward in an indeterminable pattern of cancellation and duplication. If it thus becomes impossible to determine "who started it" (or even whether "it" was started by either one of them), it is also impossible to know who is ahead or even whose "turn" it is—which is what makes the business of getting even so *odd.*

This type of oscillation between two terms, considered as totalities in binary opposition, is studied by Lacan in connection with Poe's story of the eight-year-old prodigy who succeeded in winning, far beyond his due, at the game of even and odd. The game consists of guessing whether the number of marbles an opponent is holding is even or odd. The schoolboy explains his success by his identification with the physical characteristics of his opponent, from which he deduces the opponent's degree of intelligence and its corresponding line of reasoning. What Lacan shows, in the part of his seminar which Derrida neglects, is that the mere identification with the opponent as an image of totality is not sufficient to insure success—and in no way explains Dupin's actual strategy—since, from the moment the opponent becomes aware of it, he can then play on his own appearance and dissociate it from the reasoning that is presumed to go with it. (This is, indeed, what occurs in the encounter between Dupin and the Minister: the Minister's feigned nonchalance is a true vigilance but a blinded vision, whereas Dupin's feigned blindness ["weak eyes"] is a vigilant act of lucidity, later to succumb to its own form of blindness.) From then on, says Lacan, the reasoning "can only repeat itself in an indefinite oscillation" (*Ecrits,* p. 58, translation mine). And Lacan reports that, in his own classroom tests of the schoolboy's technique, it was almost inevitable that each player begin to feel he was losing his marbles.[8]

But if the complexities of these texts could be reduced to a mere combat between ostriches, a mere game of heads and tails played out in order to determine a "winner," they would have very little theoretical interest. It is, on the contrary, the way in which each mastermind avoids simply becoming the butt of his own joke that displaces the opposition in unpredictable ways and transforms the textual encounter into a source of insight. For if the very possibility of meeting the opponent on a common ground, without which no contact is possible, implies a certain symmetry, a sameness, a repetition of the error that the encounter is designed to correct, any true avoidance of that error entails a nonmeeting or incompatibility between the two forces. If to hit the target is in a way to become the target, then to miss the target is perhaps to hit it elsewhere. It is not how Lacan and Derrida meet each other but how they miss each other that opens up a space for interpretation.

Clearly, what is at stake here has something to do with the status of the number 2. If the face-off between two opponents or polar opposites always simultaneously backfires and misfires, it can only be because 2 is an extremely "odd" number. On the one hand, as a specular illusion of symmetry or metaphor, it can be either narcissistically reassuring (the image of the other as a reinforcement of my identity) or absolutely devastating (the other whose existence can totally cancel me out). This is what Lacan calls the *"imaginary* duality." It is characterized by its absoluteness, its independence from any accident or contingency that might subvert the unity of the terms in question, whether in their opposition or in their fusion. To this, Lacan opposes the *symbolic,* which is the entrance of difference or otherness or temporality into the idea of identity—it is not something that befalls the imaginary duality, but something that has always already inhabited it, something that subverts not the symmetry of the imaginary couple, but the possibility of the independent unity of any one term whatsoever. It is the impossibility not of the number 2 but of the number 1—which, paradoxically enough, turns out to lead to the number 3.

If 3 is what makes 2 into the impossibility of 1, is there any inherent increase in lucidity in passing from a couple to a triangle? Is a triangle in any way more "true" than a couple?

It is Derrida's contention that, for psychoanalysis, the answer to that question is yes. The triangle becomes the magical, Oedipal figure that explains the functioning of human desire. The child's original imaginary dual unity with the mother is subverted by the law of the father as that which prohibits incest under threat of castration. The child has "simply" to "assume castration" as the necessity of substitution in the object of his desire (the object of desire becoming the locus of substitution and the focus of repetition), after which the child's desire becomes "normalized." Derrida's criticism of the "triangles" or "triads" in Lacan's reading of Poe is based on the assumption that Lacan's use of triangularity stems from this psychoanalytical myth.

Derrida's criticism takes two routes, both of them numerical:

1. The structure of "The Purloined Letter" cannot be reduced to a triangle unless the narrator is eliminated. The elimination of the narrator is a blatant and highly revealing result of the way "psychoanalysis" does violence to literature in order to find its own schemes. What psychoanalysis sees as a triangle is therefore really a quadrangle, and that fourth side is the point from which literature problematizes the very possibility of a triangle. Therefore: $3 = 4$.

2. Duality as such cannot be dismissed or simply absorbed into a triangular structure. "The Purloined Letter" is traversed by an uncanny capacity for doubling and subdividing. The narrator and Dupin are doubles of each other, and Dupin himself is first introduced as a "Bi-Part Soul" (Poe, p. 107), a sort of Dupin Duplex, "the creative and the resolvent." The Minister, D——, has a brother for whom it is possible to mistake him, and from whom he is to be distinguished because of his doubleness (poet and mathematician). Thus the Minister and Dupin become doubles of each other through the fact of their both being already double, in addition to their other points of resemblance, including their names. "The 'Seminar'," writes Derrida,

> mercilessly forecloses this problematic of the double and of *Unheimlichkeit*— no doubt considering that it is confined to the imaginary, to the dual relationship which must be kept rigorously separate from the symbolic and the triangular. . . . All the "uncanny" relations of duplicity, limitlessly deployed in a dual structure, find themselves omitted or marginalized [in the "Seminar"] . . . . What is thus kept under surveillance and control is the Uncanny itself, and the frantic anxiety which can be provoked, with no hope of reappropriation, enclosure, or truth, by the infinite play from simulacrum to simulacrum, from double to double. (omitted in PT; FV, P. 124, translation mine).

Thus the triangle's angles are always already bisected, and $3 =$ (a factor of) 2.

In the game of odd versus even, then, it would seem that Derrida is playing evens (4 or 2) against Lacan's odds (3). But somehow the numbers 2 and 4 have become uncannily odd, while the number 3 has been evened off into a reassuring symmetry. How did this happen, and what are the consequences for an interpretation of "The Purloined Letter"?

Before any answer to this question can be envisaged, several remarks should be made here to problematize the terms of Derrida's
critique:

1. If the narrator and Dupin are a strictly dual pair whose relationship is in no way mediated by a third term in any Oedipal sense, how is
one to explain the fact that their original meeting was brought about by
their potential rivalry over the same object: "the accident of our both
being in search of the *same* very rare and very remarkable volume"
(emphasis mine). Whether or not they ever found it, or can share it, is
this not a triangular relationship?

2. Although Lacan's reading of "The Purloined Letter" divides the
story into triadic structures, his model for (inter-)subjectivity, the so-
called schema L, which is developed in that part of the "Seminar's"
introduction glossed over by Derrida, is indisputably quadrangular. In
order to read Lacan's repeating triads as a triangular, Oedipal model
of the subject instead of as a mere structure of repetition, Derrida
must therefore lop off one corner of the schema L in the same way as
he accuses Lacan of lopping off a corner of Poe's text—and Derrida
does this by lopping off that corner of Lacan's text in which the quadrangular schema L is developed.

But can what is at stake here really be reduced to a mere numbers
game?

Let us approach the problem from another angle, by asking two
more questions:

1. What is the relation between a divided unity and a duality? Are
the two 2's synonymous? Is a "Bi-Part Soul," for example, actually
composed of two wholes? Or is it possible to conceive of a division
which would not lead to two separate parts, but only to a problematization of the idea of unity? This would class what Derrida calls "duality"
not in Lacan's "imaginary," but in Lacan's "symbolic."

2. If the doubles are forever redividing or multiplying, does the
number 2 really apply? If $1 = 2$, how can $2 = 1 + 1$? If what is uncanny
about the doubles is that they never stop doubling up, would the
number 2 still be uncanny if it did stop at a truly dual symmetry? Is
it not the very limitlessness of the process of the dissemination of
unity, rather than the existence of any one duality, which Derrida is
talking about here?

Clearly, in these questions, the very notion of a number becomes
problematic, and the argument on the basis of numbers can no longer
be read literally. If Derrida opposes doubled quadrangles to Lacan's triangles, it is not because he wants to turn Oedipus into an octopus.

To what, then, does the critique of triangularity apply?

The problem with psychoanalytical triangularity, in Derrida's eyes, is not that it contains the wrong number of terms, but that it presupposes the possibility of a successful dialectical mediation and harmonious normalization, or *Aufhebung,* of desire. The three terms in the Oedipal triad enter into an opposition whose resolution resembles the synthetic moment of a Hegelian dialectic. The process centers on the phallus as the locus of the question of sexual difference; when the observation of the mother's lack of a penis is joined with the father's threat of castration as the punishment for incest, the child passes from the alternative (thesis vs. antithesis; presence vs. absence of penis) to the synthesis (the phallus as a sign of the fact that the child can only enter into the circuit of desire by assuming castration as the phallus's simultaneous presence and absence; that is, by assuming the fact that both the subject and the object of desire will always be substitutes for something that was never really present). In Lacan's article "La signification du phallus," which Derrida quotes, this process is evoked in specifically Hegelian terms:

> All these remarks still do nothing but veil the fact that it [the phallus] cannot play its role except veiled, that is to say as itself sign of the latency with which anything signifiable is stricken as soon as it is raised (*aufgehoben*) to the function of signifier.
>
>   The phallus is the signifier of this *Aufhebung* itself which it inaugurates (initiates) by its disappearance. (*Ecrits,* P. 692; PT, P. 98.)

"It would appear," comments Derrida, "that the Hegelian movement of *Aufhebung* is here reversed since the latter sublates [relève] the sensory signifier in the ideal signified" (PT, p. 98). But then, according to Derrida, Lacan's privileging of the spoken over the written word annuls this reversal, reappropriates all possibility of uncontainable otherness, and brings the whole thing back within the bounds of the type of "logocentrism" that has been the focus of Derrida's entire deconstructive enterprise.

The question of whether or not Lacan's privileging of the voice is strictly logocentric in Derrida's sense is an extremely complex one with which we cannot hope to deal adequately here.[9] But what does all this have to do with "The Purloined Letter"?

In an attempt to answer this question, let us examine how Derrida deduces from Lacan's text that, for Lacan, the letter is a symbol of the (mother's) phallus. Since Lacan never uses the word *phallus* in the "Seminar," this is already an interpretation on Derrida's part, and quite an astute one at that, with which Lacan, as a later reader of his own

"Seminar," implicitly agrees by placing the word *castrated*—which had not been used in the original text—in his "Points" *Presentation*. The disagreement between Derrida and Lacan thus arises not over the *validity* of the equation "letter = phallus," but over its *meaning*.

How, then, does Derrida derive this equation from Lacan's text? The deduction follows four basic lines of reasoning, all of which will be dealt with in greater detail later in the present essay:

1. The letter "belongs" to the Queen as a substitute for the phallus she does not have. It feminizes (castrates) each of its successive holders and is eventually returned to her as its rightful owner.

2. Poe's description of the position of the letter in the Minister's apartment, expanded upon by the figurative dimensions of Lacan's text, suggests an analogy between the shape of the fireplace from the center of whose mantelpiece the letter is found hanging and that point on a woman's anatomy from which the phallus is missing.

3. The letter, says Lacan, cannot be divided: "But if it is first of all on the materiality of the signifier that we have insisted, that materiality is *odd* [singulière] in many ways, the first of which is not to admit partition" (SPL, p. 53). This indivisibility, says Derrida, is odd indeed, but becomes comprehensible if it is seen as an *idealization* of the phallus, whose integrity is necessary for the edification of the entire psychoanalytical system. With the phallus safely idealized and located in the voice, the so-called signifier acquires the "unique, living, non-mutilable integrity" of the self-present spoken word, unequivocally pinned down to and by the *signified*. "Had the phallus been per(mal)-chance divisible or reduced to the status of a partial object, the whole edification would have crumbled down, and this is what has to be avoided at all cost" (PT, pp. 96-97).

4. And finally, if Poe's story "illustrates" the "truth," the last words of the "Seminar" proper seem to reaffirm that truth in no uncertain terms: "Thus it is that what the 'purloined letter,' nay the 'letter in sufferance' means is that *a letter always arrives at its destination*" (SPL, p. 72, emphasis mine). Now, since it is unlikely that Lacan is talking about the efficiency of the postal service, he must, according to Derrida, be affirming the possibility of unequivocal meaning, the eventual reappropriation of the message, its total equivalence with itself. And since the "truth" Poe's story illustrates is, in Derrida's eyes, the truth of veiled/unveiled castration and of the transcendental identity of the phallus as the lack that makes the system work, this final sentence in Lacan's "Seminar" seems to affirm both the absolute truth of psychoanalytical theories and the absolute decipherability of the

literary text. Poe's message will have been totally, unequivocally understood and explained by the psychoanalytical myth. "The hermeneutic
discovery of meaning (truth), the deciphering (that of Dupin and that
of the "Seminar"), arrives itself at its destination" (PT, p. 66).

Thus, the law of the phallus seems to imply a reappropriating return
to the place of true ownership, an indivisible identity functioning
beyond the possibility of disintegration or unrecoverable loss, and a
totally self-present, unequivocal meaning or truth.

The problem with this type of system, counters Derrida, is that it
cannot account for the possibility of sheer accident, irreversible loss,
unreappropriable residues, and infinite divisibility, which are necessary
and inevitable in the system's very elaboration. In order for the circuit
of the letter to end up confirming the law of the phallus, it must begin
by transgressing it; the letter is a sign of high treason. Phallogocentrism
mercilessly represses the uncontrollable multiplicity of ambiguities, the
disseminating play of *writing,* which irreducibly transgresses any unequivocal meaning. "Not that the letter never arrives at its destination,
but part of its structure is that it is always capable of not arriving
there. . . . Here dissemination threatens the law of the signifier and of
castration as a contract of truth. Dissemination mutilates the unity of
the signifier, that is, of the phallus" (PT, p. 66).

In contrast to Lacan's "Seminar", then, Derrida's text would seem
to be setting itself up as a "Disseminar."

From the foregoing remarks, it can easily be seen that the disseminal criticism of Lacan's apparent reduction of the literary text to an
unequivocal message depends for its force upon the presupposition of
unambiguousness in Lacan's text. And indeed, the statement that a
letter always reaches its destination seems straightforward enough.
But when the statement is reinserted into its context, things become
palpably less certain:

> Is that all, and shall we believe we have deciphered Dupin's real strategy
> above and beyond the imaginary tricks upon which he was obliged to deceive
> us? No doubt, yes, for if "any point requiring reflection," as Dupin states at
> the start, is "examined to best purpose in the dark," we may now easily read
> its solution in broad daylight. It was already implicit and easy to derive from
> the title of our tale, according to the very formula we have long submitted to
> your discretion: in which the sender, we tell you, receives from the receiver
> his own message in reverse form. Thus it is that what the "purloined letter,"
> nay, the "letter in sufferance" means is that a letter always arrives at its des-
> tination. (SPL, p. 72.)

The meaning of this last sentence is problematized not so much by its own ambiguity as by a series of reversals in the preceding sentences. If the "best" examination takes place in darkness, what does "reading in broad daylight" imply? Could it not be taken as an affirmation not of actual lucidity but of delusions of lucidity? Could it not then move the "yes, no doubt" as an answer, not to the question, Have we deciphered? but to the question, Shall we *believe* we have deciphered? And if this is possible, does it not empty the final affirmation of all unequivocality, leaving it to stand with the *force* of an assertion, without any definite content? And if the sender receives from the receiver his own message backward, who is the sender here, who the receiver, and what is the message? It is not even clear what the expression "the purloined letter" refers to: Poe's text? the letter it talks about? or simply the expression "the purloined letter"?

We will take another look at this passage later, but for the moment its ambiguities seem sufficient to problematize, if not subvert, the presupposition of univocality that is the very foundation on which Derrida has edified his interpretation.

But surely such an oversimplification on Derrida's part does not result from mere blindness, oversight, or error. As Paul de Man says of Derrida's similar treatment of Rousseau, "the pattern is too interesting not to be deliberate."[10] Derrida being the sharp-eyed reader that he is, his consistent forcing of Lacan's statements into systems and patterns from which they are actually trying to escape must correspond to some strategic necessity different from the attentiveness to the letter of the text which characterizes Derrida's way of reading Poe. And in fact, the more one works with Derrida's analysis, the more convinced one becomes that although the critique of what Derrida calls psychoanalysis is entirely justified, it does not quite apply to what Lacan's text is actually saying. Derrida argues, in effect, not against Lacan's *text* but against Lacan's *power*—or rather, against "Lacan" as the apparent cause of certain effects of power in French discourse today. Whatever Lacan's text may *say*, it functions, according to Derrida, as if it said what *he* says it says. The statement that a letter always reaches its destination may be totally undecipherable, but its assertive force is taken all the more seriously as a sign that Lacan himself has everything all figured out. Such an assertion, in fact, gives him an appearance of mastery like that of the Minister in the eyes of the letterless Queen. "The ascendancy which the Minister derives from the situation," explains Lacan, "is attached not to the letter but to the character it makes him into."

Thus Derrida's seemingly "blind" reading, whose vagaries we shall be following here, is not a mistake, but the positioning of what can be called the "average reading" of Lacan's text—the true object of Derrida's deconstruction. Since Lacan's text is read as if it said what Derrida says it says, its actual textual functioning is irrelevant to the agonistic arena in which Derrida's analysis takes place and which is suggested by the very first word of the epigraph: *ils* (they):

> They thank him for the grand truths he has just proclaimed,—for they have discovered (o verifier of what cannot be verified) that everything he said was absolutely true; even though, at first, these honest souls admit, they might have suspected that it could have been a simple fiction . . . (PT, P. 31; translation mine.)

The fact that this quotation from Baudelaire refers to Poe and not Lacan does not completely erase the impression that the unidentified "him" in its first sentence is the "Purveyor of Truth" of the title. The evils of Lacan's analysis of Poe are thus located less in the letter of the text than in the gullible readers, the "braves gens" who are taken in by it. Lacan's ills are really *ils*.

If Derrida's reading of Lacan's reading of Poe is actually the deconstruction of a reading whose status is difficult to determine, does this mean that Lacan's text is completely innocent of the misdemeanors of which it is accused? If Lacan can be shown to be opposed to the same kind of logocentric error that Derrida opposes, does that mean that they are both really saying the same thing? These are questions that must be left, at least for the moment, hanging.

But the structure of Derrida's transference of guilt from a certain reading of Lacan onto Lacan's text is not indifferent in itself, in the context of what, after all, started out as a relatively simple crime story. For what it amounts to is nothing less than a *frame*.

The Frame of Reference

> Elle, défunte *nue* en le miroir, encor
> Que, *dans l'oubli fermé par le cadre*, se fixe
> De scintillations sitôt le septuor.
>
> —Mallarmé, "Sonnet en X"

If Derrida is thus framing Lacan for an interpretative malpractice of which he himself is, at least in part, the author, what can this frame teach us about the nature of the act of reading, in the context of the question of literature and psychoanalysis?

Interestingly enough, one of the major crimes for which Derrida frames Lacan is the psychoanalytical reading's elimination of the literary text's *frame*. That frame here consists not only of the two stories that precede "The Purloined Letter" but also of the stratum of narration

through which the stories are told, and, "beyond" it, of the text's
entire functioning as *écriture:*

> Without breathing a word about it, Lacan excludes the textual fiction with-
> in which he isolates the so-called "general narration." Such an operation is
> facilitated, too obviously facilitated, by the fact that the narration covers the
> entire surface of the fiction entitled "The Purloined Letter." But *that* is the
> fiction. There is an invisible but structurally irreducible frame around the
> narration. Where does it begin? With the first letter of the title? With the
> epigraph from Seneca? With the words, "At Paris, just after dark . . ."? It is
> more complicated than that and will require reconsideration. Such complica-
> tion suffices to point out everything that is misunderstood about the structure
> of the text once the frame is ignored. Within this invisible or neutralized frame,
> Lacan takes the borderless narration and makes another subdivision, once
> again leaving aside the frame. He cuts out two dialogues from within the frame
> of the narration itself, which form the narrated history, i.e. the content of a
> representation, the internal meaning of a story, the all-enframed which de-
> mands our complete attention, mobilizes all the psychoanalytical schemes—
> Oedipal, as it happens—and draws all the effort of decipherment towards its
> center. What is missing here is an elaboration of the problem of the frame, the
> signature and the *parergon.* This lack allows us to reconstruct the scene of the
> signifier as a signified (an ever inevitable process in the logic of the sign), writ-
> ing as the written, the text as discourse or more precisely as an "intersubjec-
> tive" dialogue (there is nothing fortuitous in the fact that the Seminar discusses
> only the two *dialogues* in "The Purloined Letter"). (PT, pp. 52–53, translation
> modified.)

> It is well known that "The Purloined Letter" belongs to what Baudelaire
> called a "kind of trilogy," along with "The Murders in the Rue Morgue" and
> "The Mystery of Marie Rogêt." About this Dupin trilogy, the Seminar does not
> breathe a word; not only does Lacan lift out the narrated triangles (the "real
> drama") in order to center the narration around them and make them carry the
> weight of the interpretation (the letter's destination), but he also lifts one third
> of the Dupin cycle out of an ensemble discarded as if it were a natural, invisible
> frame. (Not translated in PT; FV, p. 123; translation mine.)

> In framing with such violence, in cutting a fourth side out of the narrated
> figure itself in order to see only triangles, a certain complication, perhaps a
> complication of the Oedipal structure, is eluded, a complication which makes
> itself felt in the scene of writing. (PT, p. 54; translation entirely modified.)

It would seem, then, that Lacan is guilty of several sins of omission:
the omission of the narrator, the nondialogue parts of the story, the
other stories in the trilogy. But does this criticism amount to a mere
plea for the inclusion of what has been excluded? No; the problem is
not simply quantitative. What has been excluded is not homogeneous to
what has been included. Lacan, says Derrida, misses the specifically
literary dimension of Poe's text by treating it as a "real drama," a story

like the stories a psychoanalyst hears every day from his patients. What
has been left out is literature itself.

Does this mean that the frame is what makes a text literary? In an
issue of *New Literary History* devoted to the question "What is literature?" (and totally unrelated to the debate concerning the purloined
letter) one of the contributors comes to this very conclusion: "Literature is language . . . but it is language around which we have drawn a
frame, a frame that indicates a decision to regard with a particular self-
consciousness the resources language has always possessed"[11] (emphasis
mine).

Such a view of literature, however, implies that a text is literary
because it remains inside certain definite borders; it is a many-faceted
object, perhaps, but still, it is an object. That this is not quite what
Derrida has in mind becomes clear from the following remarks:

> By overlooking the narrator's position, the narrator's involvement in the
> content of what he seems to be recounting, one omits from the scene of
> writing anything going beyond the two triangular scenes.
> And first of all one omits that what is in question—with no possible access
> route or border—is a scene of writing whose boundaries crumble off into an
> abyss. From the simulacrum of an overture, of a "first word," the narrator, in
> narrating himself, advances a few propositions which carry the unity of the
> "tale" into an endless drifting-off course: a textual drifting not at all taken
> into account in the Seminar. (PT, pp. 100–101; translation modified.)

> These reminders, of which countless other examples could be given, alert us
> to the effects of the frame, and of the paradoxes in the parergonal logic. Our
> purpose is not to prove that "The Purloined Letter" functions within a frame
> (omitted by the Seminar, which can thus be assured of its triangular interior
> by an active, surreptitious limitation starting from a metalinguistic overview),
> but to prove that the structure of the framing effects is such that no totaliza-
> tion of the border is even possible. Frames are always framed: thus, by part of
> their content. Pieces without a whole, "divisions" without a totality—this is
> what thwarts the dream of a letter without division, allergic to division. (PT,
> p. 99; translation slightly modified.)

Here the argument seems to reverse the previous objection; Lacan
has eliminated not the frame but the unframability of the literary text.
But what Derrida calls "parergonal logic" is paradoxical precisely because both of these incompatible (but not totally contradictory) arguments are equally valid. The total inclusion of the frame is both
mandatory and impossible. The frame thus becomes not the borderline
between the inside and the outside, but precisely what subverts the
applicability of the inside/outside polarity to the act of interpretation.

The frame is, in fact, one of a series of paradoxical "borderline
cases"—along with the tympanum and the hymen—through which

Derrida has recently been studying the limits of spatial logic as it relates to intelligibility. Lacan, too, has been seeking to displace the Euclidean model of understanding (comprehension, for example, means spatial inclusion) by inventing a "new geometry" by means of the logic of knots. The relation between these two attempts to break out of spatial logic has yet to be articulated, but some measure of the difficulties involved may be derived from the fact that *to break out of* is still a spatial metaphor. The urgency of these undertakings cannot, however, be over-estimated, since the logic of metaphysics, of politics, of belief, and of knowledge itself is based on the imposition of definable objective frontiers and outlines whose possibility and/or justifiability are here being put in question. If "comprehension" is the framing of something whose limits are undeterminable, how can we know what we are comprehending? The play on the spatial and the criminal senses of the word *frame* with which we began this section may thus not be as gratuitous as it seemed. And indeed, the question of the fallacies inherent in a Euclidean model of intelligibility, far from being a tangential theoretical consideration here, is central to the very plot of "The Purloined Letter" itself. For it is precisely the notion of space as finite and homogeneous that underlies the Prefect's method of investigation: "I presume you know," he explains, "that, to a properly trained police-agent, such a thing as a 'secret' drawer is impossible. Any man is a dolt who permits a 'secret' drawer to escape him in a search of this kind. The thing is *so* plain. There is a certain amount of bulk—of space—to be accounted for in every cabinet. Then we have accurate rules. The fiftieth part of a line could not escape us" (Poe, p. 204). The assumption that what is not seen must be hidden—an assumption Lacan calls the "realist's imbecillity"—is based on a falsely objective notion of the act of *seeing*. The polarity "hidden/exposed" cannot alone account for the police's *not* finding the letter—which was entirely exposed, inside out—let alone for Dupin's finding it. A "subjective" element must be added, which subverts the geometrical model of understanding through the interference of the polarity "blindness/sight" with the polarity "hidden/exposed." The same problematic is raised by the story of "The Emperor's New Clothes," which Derrida cites as an example of psychoanalysis' failure to go beyond the polarity "hidden/exposed" (in Freud's account). We will return to the letter's "place" later on in this essay, but it is already clear that the "range" of any investigation is located not in geometrical space, but in its implicit notion of what "seeing" is.

What enables Derrida to problematize the literary text's frame is, as we have seen, what he calls "the scene of writing." By this he means two things.

1. *The textual signifier's resistance to being totally transformed into a signified.* In spite of Lacan's attentiveness to the path of the letter in Poe's story as an illustration of the functioning of a signifier, says Derrida, the psychoanalytical reading is still blind to the functioning of the signifier in the narration itself. In reading "The Purloined Letter" as an allegory of the signifier, Lacan, according to Derrida, has made the "signifier" into the story's truth: "The displacement of the signifier is analyzed as a signified, as the recounted object in a short story" (PT, p. 48). Whereas, counters Derrida, it is precisely the textual signifier that resists being thus totalized into meaning, leaving an irreducible residue: "The rest, the remnant, would be 'The Purloined Letter,' the text that bears this title, and whose place, like the once more invisible large letters on the map, is not where one was expecting to find it, in the enclosed content of the 'real drama' or in the hidden and sealed interior of Poe's story, but in and as the open letter, the very open letter which fiction is" (PT, p. 64).

2. *The actual writings*—the books, libraries, quotations, and previous tales that surround "The Purloined Letter" with a frame of (literary) references. The story begins in "a little back library, or book-closet" (Poe, p. 199), where the narrator is mulling over a previous conversation on the subject of the two previous instances of Dupin's detective work as told in Poe's two previous tales, the first of which recounted the original meeting between Dupin and the narrator—in a library, of course, where both were in search of the same rare book. The story's beginning is thus an infinitely regressing reference to previous writings. And therefore, says Derrida, "nothing begins. Simply a drifting or a disorientation from which one never moves away" (PT, p. 101). Dupin, himself, is in fact a walking library; books are his "sole luxuries," and the narrator is "astonished" at "the vast extent of his reading" (Poe, p. 106). Even Dupin's last, most seemingly personal words—the venomous lines he leaves in his substitute letter to the Minister—are a quotation, whose transcription and proper authorship are the last things the story tells us. "But," concludes Derrida, "beyond the quotation marks that surround the entire story, Dupin is obliged to quote this last word in quotation marks, to recount his signature: that is what I wrote to him and how I signed it. What is a signature within quotation marks? Then, within these quotation marks, the seal itself is a quotation within quotation marks. This remnant is still literature" (PT, pp. 112-13).

It is by means of these two extra dimensions that Derrida intends to show the crumbling, abyssal, nontotalizable edges of the story's frame.

Both of these objections, however, are in themselves more problematic and double-edged than they appear. Let us begin with the second. "Literature" in Derrida's demonstration is indeed clearly the beginning, middle, and end—and even the interior—of the purloined letter. But how was this conclusion reached? To a large extent, by listing the books, libraries, and other writings recounted in the story. That is, by following the theme—and not the functioning—of "writing" within "the content of a representation." But if Dupin's signing with a quotation, for example, is for Derrida a sign that "this remnant is still literature," does this not indicate that "literature" has become not the signifier but the signified in the story? If the play of the signifier is really to be followed, does it not play beyond the range of the *seme* "writing"? And if Derrida criticizes Lacan for making the "signifier" into the story's signified, is Derrida not here transforming "writing" into "the written" in much the same way? What Derrida calls "the reconstruction of the scene of the signifier as a signified" seems indeed to be "an inevitable process" in the logic of reading the purloined letter.

Derrida, of course, implicitly counters this objection by protesting—twice—that the textual drifting for which Lacan does not account should not be considered "the *real subject* of the tale," but rather the "remarkable ellipsis" of any subject (PT, p. 102). But the question of the seemingly inevitable slipping from the signifier to the signified still remains, and not as an objection to the logic of the frame, but as its fundamental question. For if the "paradoxes of parergonal logic" are such that the frame is always being framed by part of its contents, it is this very slippage between signifier and signified, *acted out* by both Derrida and Lacan against their intentions, which best illustrates those paradoxes. Derrida's justification of his framing of the "Lacan" he is reading as neither being limited to the "Seminar" nor as including Lacan's later work, itself obeys the contradictory logic of the frame. On the one hand, Derrida will study that part of Lacan's work which seems to embody a system of truth even though other writings might put that system in question, and on the other hand this same part of Lacan's work, says Derrida, will probably some day be called the work of the "young Lacan" by "academics eager to divide up *what cannot be divided*" (PT, p. 82, translation modified). Whatever Derrida actually thinks he is doing here, his contradictory way of explaining it obeys the paradoxes of parergonal logic so perfectly that this self-subversion may have even been deliberate.

If the question of the frame thus problematizes the object of any interpretation by setting it at an angle or fold (*pli*) with itself, then Derrida's analysis errs not in opposing this paradoxical functioning to

Lacan's allegorical reading, but in not following the consequences of its own insight far enough. For example, if it is the frame that makes it impossible for us to know where to begin and when to stop, why does Derrida stop within the limits of the Dupin trilogy? And if the purpose of studying "writing" is to sow an uncanny uncertainty about our position in the abyss, is not the disseminal library Derrida describes still in a way just a bit too comfortable?

"The Purloined Letter," says Derrida, is signed "literature." What does this mean, if not that the letter's contents—the only ones we are allowed to see—are in another text? That the locus of the letter's meaning is not in the letter, but somewhere else? That the context of that meaning is the way in which its context is lacking, both through the explicit designation of a proper origin (Crébillon's *Atrée*) *outside* the text and through a substitutive structure from letter to letter, from text to text, and from brother to brother, *within* the text, such that the expressions *outside* and *within* have ceased to be clearly definable? But until we have actually opened that other text, we cannot know the modality of the precise otherness of the abyss to itself, the way in which the story's edges do not simply crumble away.

In order to escape the reduction of the "library" to its thematic presence as a *sign* of writing, let us therefore pull some of the books off the shelves and see what they contain. This is a track neither Lacan nor Derrida has taken, but we will soon see how it in some way enfolds them both.

First of all, the name *Dupin* itself, according to Poe scholars, comes out of Poe's interior library: from the pages of a volume called *Sketches of Conspicuous Living Characters of France* (Philadelphia: Lea & Blanchard, 1841), which Poe reviewed for *Graham's Magazine* during the same month his first Dupin story appeared. André-Marie-Jean-Jacques Dupin, a minor French statesman, is there described as himself a walking library: "To judge from his writings, Dupin must be a perfect living encyclopedia. From Homer to Rousseau, from the Bible to the civil code, from the laws of the twelve tables to the Koran, he has read every thing, retained every thing . . ." (p. 224). Detective Dupin's "origin" is thus multiply bookish. He is a reader whose writer read his name in a book describing a writer as a reader—a reader whose nature can only be described in writing, in fact, as irreducibly double: "He is the personage for whom the painters of political portraits, make the most enormous consumption of antithesis. In the same picture, he will be drawn as both great and little, courageous and timid, trivial and dignified, disinterested and mercenary, restive and pliable, obstinate and fickle, white and black; there is no understanding it" (p. 210). And the writing that serves as the vehicle of this description of written descriptions of double Dupin is itself double: a translation, by a Mr. Walsh, of a series of articles by a Frenchman whose name is not even known to the translator but who is said to call himself "an *homme de rien,* a nobody" (p. 2). "Nobody" thus becomes the proper name of the original author in the series.[12]

But the author of the last word in "The Purloined Letter" is clearly *not* nobody. It is not even Poe; it is Crébillon. When read as the context from which Dupin's letter to the Minister has been purloined, Crébillon's *Atrée* is remarkable not simply because it tells the story of revenge as a symmetrical repetition of the original crime, but because it does so precisely by means of a purloined letter. A *letter* informs King Atreus of the extent of his betrayal and serves as an instrument of his revenge; the King himself has purloined the letter—written by the Queen to her lover, Thyestes, just before her death. The letter reveals that Plisthenes, whom everyone believes to be Atreus's son, is really the son of his brother Thyestes. Having kept the letter and its message secret for twenty years, Atreus plans to force Plisthenes, unaware of his true parentage, to commit patricide. Thwarted in this plan by Plisthenes's refusal to kill the father of his beloved, Theodamia, who is, unknown to him, his sister, Atreus is forced to produce the letter, reunite the illicit family, and transfer his revenge from Plisthenes's patricide to Thyestes's infantophagy. A Queen betraying a King, a letter representing that betrayal being purloined for purposes of power, an eventual return of that letter to its addressee, accompanied by an act of revenge which duplicates the original crime—"The Purloined Letter" as a story of repetition is itself a repetition of the story from which it purloins its last words. The Freudian "truth" of the repetition compulsion is not simply illustrated *in* the story; it is illustrated *by* the story. The story obeys the very law it conveys; it is framed by its own content. And thus "The Purloined Letter" no longer simply repeats its own "primal scene": what it repeats is nothing less than a previous story of repetition. The "last word" names the place where the "nonfirstness" of the "first word" repeats itself.

This is not the only instance of the folding-in of the frame of references upon the purloined letter's interior. Another allusion, somewhat more hidden, is contained in the description of the Minister as someone "who dares all things, those unbecoming as well as those becoming a man" (Poe, p. 201). These words echo Macbeth's protestation to his ambitious wife: "I dare do all that may become a man./Who dares do more is none" (1,7). The reference to *Macbeth* substantiates Lacan's reading of the description of the Minister as pointing toward femininity;

it is indeed Lady Macbeth who dares to do what is unbecoming a man. And what is Lady Macbeth doing when we first catch sight of her? She is reading a letter. Not a purloined letter, perhaps, but one that contains the ambiguous letter of destiny, committing Macbeth to the murder of the King, whose place Macbeth will take and whose fate he will inevitably share. Kings seem to be unable to remain unscathed in the face of a letter—Atreus betrayed by his wife's letter to his brother; Duncan betrayed by Macbeth's letter to Lady Macbeth; Macbeth himself betrayed by his own confidence in his ability to read the letter of his Fate; and of course, the King in "The Purloined Letter," whose power is betrayed by his not even knowing about the existence of the letter that betrays him.

The questions raised by all these texts together are legion. What is a man? Who is the child's father? What is the relation between incest, murder, and the death of a child? What is a king? How can we read the letter of our destiny? What is seeing? The crossroads where these stories come together seems to point to the story of what occurred at another crossroads: the tragedy of Oedipus the King. We seem to have returned to our starting point, then, except for one thing: it is no longer "The Purloined Letter" that repeats the story of Oedipus, but the story of Oedipus that repeats all the letters purloined from "The Purloined Letter"'s abyssal interior.

But the letter does not stop there. For the very Oedipal reading that Derrida attributes to Lacan is itself, according to Derrida, a purloined letter—purloined by Lacan from Marie Bonaparte's psychobiographical study of the life and works of Edgar Allan Poe: "At the moment when the Seminar, like Dupin, finds the letter where it is to be found, between the legs of the woman, the deciphering of the enigma is anchored in truth. . . . Why then does it find, at the same time that it finds truth, the same meaning and the same topos as Bonaparte when, leaping over the text, she proposes a psycho-biographical analysis of 'The Purloined Letter'?" (PT, p. 66). In that analysis, Bonaparte sees Dupin's restitution of the letter to the Queen as the return of the missing maternal penis to the mother. The letter's hiding place in the Minister's apartment, moreover, is "almost an anatomical chart" of the female body— which leads Bonaparte to note that Baudelaire's translation of "hung from a little brass knob just beneath the middle of the mantelpiece" as "suspendu à un petit bouton de cuivre—au dessus du manteau de la cheminée" ("*above* the mantelpiece") is "completely wrong" (quoted in PT, p. 68). Bonaparte's frame of reference—the female body—cannot tolerate this error of translation.

A note that Lacan drops on the subject of the letter's position enables Derrida to frame Lacan for neglecting to mention his references: "The question of deciding," says Lacan, "whether he [Dupin] seizes it [the letter] above the mantelpiece as Baudelaire translates, or beneath it, as in the original text, may be abandoned without harm to the inferences of those whose profession is grilling [aux inférences de la cuisine]." Lacan's note: "And even to the cook herself" (SPL, pp. 66–67). In this cavalier treatment of Bonaparte as the "cook," Lacan thus "makes clear" to Derrida "that Lacan had read Bonaparte, although the Seminar never alludes to her. As an author so careful about debts and priorities, he could have acknowledged an irruption that orients his entire interpretation, namely, the process of rephallization as the proper course of the letter, the 'return of the letter' restored to its 'destination' after having been found between the legs of the mantelpiece" (PT, p. 68). The interpretation of the letter (as the phallus that must be returned to the mother) must itself be returned to the "mother" from whom it has been purloined—Marie Bonaparte. Derrida thus follows precisely the logic he objects to in Lacan, the logic of rectification and correction: "to return the letter to its proper course, supposing that its trajectory is a line, is to correct a deviation, to rectify a divergence, to recall a direction, an authentic line" (PT, p. 65). But the mere fact that Derrida's critique repeats the same logic he denounces is in itself less interesting than the fact that this rectification presupposes another, which puts its very foundations in question. For when Lacan says that the question of the exact position of the letter "may be abandoned without harm" to the grillers, Derrida protests, "Without harm? On the contrary, the harm would be decisive, within the Seminar itself: *on* the mantelpiece, the letter could not have been 'between the cheeks of the fireplace,' 'between the legs of the fireplace'" (PT, p. 69). Derrida must thus correct Lacan's text, eliminate its apparent contradiction, in order to return the letter of interpretation to its rightful owner. And all this in order to criticize Lacan's enterprise as one of rectification and circular return. If "rectification" as such is to be criticized, it is difficult to determine where it begins and where it ends. In rectifying Lacan's text in order to make it fit into the logic of rectification, Derrida thus problematizes the very status of the object of his criticism.

But if the correction of Lacan's text is itself a mutilation that requires correction, how *are* we to interpret the contradiction between Lacan's description of the Minister's apartment as "an immense female body" (SPL, p. 66) and his statement that the letter's exact location does not matter? This, it seems to me, is the crux of the divergence between Derrida's and Lacan's interpretation of what the equation "letter = phallus" means.

For Bonaparte, it was precisely the analogy between the fireplace and the female body which led to the letter's phallic function. The phallus was considered as a real, anatomical referent serving as the model for a figurative representation. Bonaparte's frame of reference was thus *reference* itself.

For Derrida, on the other hand, the phallus's frame of reference is "psychoanalytical theory"'s way of preserving the phallus's referential status in the act of negating it. In commenting on Lacan's discussion of "The Meaning of the Phallus," Derrida writes:

> Phallogocentrism is one thing. And what is called man and what is called woman might be subject to it. The more so, we are reminded, since the phallus is neither a phantasy ("imaginary effect") nor an object ("partial, internal, good, bad"), even less the organ, penis or clitoris, which it symbolizes [Ecrits, p. 690]. Androcentrism ought therefore to be something else.
>
> Yet what is going on? The entire phallogocentrism is articulated from the starting-point of a determinate *situation* (let us give this word its full impact) in which the phallus *is* the mother's desire inasmuch as she does not have it. An (individual, perceptual, local, cultural, historical, etc.) situation on the basis of which is developed something called a "sexual theory": in it the phallus is not the organ, penis or clitoris, which it symbolizes; but it does to a larger extent and in the first place symbolize the penis. . . . This consequence had to be traced in order to recognize the meaning [the direction, *sens*] of the purloined letter in the "course *which is proper to it.*" (PT, pp. 98-99).

Thus, says Derrida, the very nonreferentiality of the phallus, in the final analysis, insures that the penis is its referent.

Before trying to determine the applicability of this summary to Lacan's actual statements in "The Meaning of the Phallus"—not to mention in the "Seminar"—let us follow its consequences further in Derrida's critique. From the very first words of "The Purveyor of Truth," psychoanalysis is implicitly being criticized for being capable of finding only itself wherever it looks: "Psychoanalysis, supposing, finds itself" (PT, p. 31, translation mine.) In whatever it turns its attention to, psychoanalysis seems to recognize nothing but its own (Oedipal) schemes. Dupin finds the letter because "he knows that the letter finally *finds itself* where it must *be found* in order to return circularly and adequately to its proper place. This proper place, known to Dupin and to the psychoanalyst who intermittently takes his place, is the place of castration" (PT, p. 60; translation modified). The psychoanalyst's act, then, is one of mere *recognition* of the expected, a recognition that Derrida finds explicitly stated as such by Lacan in the underlined words he quotes from the "Seminar": "Just so does the purloined letter, like an immense female body, stretch out across the Minister's office when Dupin enters. But just so does he already *expect to find it* [emphasis mine—J.D.] and has only, with his eyes veiled by green lenses, to undress that huge body" (PT, pp. 61-62; emphasis and brackets in original).

But if recognition is a form of blindness, a form of violence to the otherness of the object, it would seem that, by eliminating Lacan's suggestion of a possible complication of the phallic scheme, and by lying in wait between the brackets of the fireplace to catch the psychoanalyst at his own game, Derrida, too, is "recognizing" rather than reading. He recognizes, as he himself says, a certain classical conception of psychoanalysis: "From the beginning," writes Derrida early in his study, *"we recognize* the classical landscape of applied psychoanalysis" (PT, p. 45; emphasis mine). It would seem that the theoretical frame of reference which governs recognition is a constitutive element in the blindness of any interpretative insight. That frame of reference allows the analyst to frame the author of the text he is reading for practices whose locus is simultaneously beyond the letter of the text and behind the vision of its reader. The reader is framed by his own frame, but he is not even in possession of his own guilt, since it is that which prevents his vision from coinciding with itself. Just as the author of a criminal frame transfers guilt from himself to another by leaving *signs* that he hopes will be read as insufficiently erased traces or referents left by the other, the author of any critique is himself framed by his own frame of the other, no matter how guilty or innocent the other may be.

What is at stake here is therefore the question of the relation between referentiality and interpretation. And here we find an interesting twist: while criticizing Lacan's notion of the phallus as being too referential, Derrida goes on to use referential logic against it. This comes up in connection with the letter's famous "materiality," which Derrida finds so odd. "It would be hard to exaggerate here the scope of this proposition on the indivisibility of the letter, or rather on its identity to itself inaccessible to dismemberment . . . as well as on the so-called materiality of the signifier (the letter) intolerant to partition. But where does this idea come from? A torn-up letter may be purely and simply destroyed, it happens . . ." (PT, pp. 86-87; translation modified). The so-called materiality of the signifier, says Derrida, is nothing but an *idealization.*

But what if the signifier were precisely what put the polarity "materiality/ideality" in question? Has it not become obvious that neither Lacan's description ("Tear a letter into little pieces, it remains the letter that it is") nor Derrida's description ("A torn-up letter may be purely and simply destroyed, it happens . . .") can be read literally? Somehow, a rhetorical fold (*pli*) in the text is there to trip us up whichever way we turn. Especially since the expression "it happens" (*ça arrive*) uses the very word on which the controversy over the letter's *arrival* at its destination turns.

Our study of the readings of "The Purloined Letter" has thus brought us to the point where the word *letter* no longer has any literality. But what is a letter that has no literality?

A "Pli" for Understanding

> I pull in resolution, and begin
> To doubt the equivocation of the fiend
> That lies like truth.
> > —Macbeth
>
> "Why do you lie to me saying you're going to Cracow so I should believe you're going to Lemberg, when in reality you *are* going to Cracow?"
> > —Joke quoted by Lacan after Freud

The letter, then, poses the question of its own rhetorical status. It moves rhetorically through the two long, minute studies in which it is presumed to be the literal object of analysis, without having any literality. Instead of simply being explained by those analyses, the rhetoric of the letter problematizes the very rhetorical mode of analytical discourse. And if *literal* means "to the letter," the literal becomes the most problematically figurative mode of all.

As the locus of rhetorical displacement, the letter made its very entrance into Poe's story by "traumatizing" the Prefect's discourse about it. After a series of paradoxes and pleas for absolute secrecy, the Prefect describes the problem created by the letter with a proliferation of *periphrases* which the narrator dubs "the cant of diplomacy":

> "Well, then; I have received personal information, from a very high quarter, that a certain document of the last importance has been purloined from the royal apartments. The individual who purloined it is known; this beyond a doubt; he was seen to take it. It is known, also, that it still remains in his possession."
>
> "How is this known?" asked Dupin.
>
> "It is clearly inferred," replied the Prefect, "from the nature of the document, and from the non-appearance of certain results which would at once arise from its passing *out* of the robber's possession—that is to say, from his employing it as he must design in the end to employ it."
>
> "Be a little more explicit," I said.
>
> "Well, I may venture so far as to say that the paper gives its holder a certain power in a certain quarter where such power is immensely valuable." The Prefect was fond of the cant of diplomacy. (Poe, P. 200.)

The letter thus enters the discourse of Poe's story as a rhetorical fold that actually hides nothing, since, although *we* never find out what was written in the letter, presumably the Queen, the Minister, Dupin, the Prefect—who all held the letter in their hands—and even the narrator, who heard what the Prefect read from his memorandum-book, *did*. The way in which the letter dictates a series of circumlocutions, then, resembles the way in which the path of the letter dictates the characters' circumvolutions—not that the letter's contents *must* remain hidden, but that the question of whether or not they are revealed is immaterial to the displacement the letter governs. The character and actions of each of the letter's holders are determined by the rhetorical spot it puts them in *whether or not* that spot can be read by the subjects it displaces.

The letter, then, acts as a signifier *not* because its contents are lacking, but because its function is not dependent on the knowledge or nonknowledge of those contents. Therefore, by saying that the letter cannot be divided Lacan does not mean that the phallus must remain intact, but that the phallus, the letter, and the signifier *are not substances*. The letter cannot be divided because it only functions *as* a division. It is not something with "an *identity* to itself inaccessible to dismemberment" (PT, pp. 86–87, emphasis mine) as Derrida interprets it; it is a *difference*. It is known only in its effects. The signifier is an articulation in a chain, not an identifiable unit. It cannot be known in itself because it is capable of "sustaining itself *only* in a displacement" (SPL, p. 59; emphasis mine). It is localized, but only as the nongeneralizable locus of a differential relationship. Derrida, in fact, enacts this law of the signifier in the very act of opposing it:

> Perhaps only one letter need be changed, maybe even less than a letter in the expression: "missing from its place [*manque à sa place*]. Perhaps we need only introduce a written "a," i.e. without accent, in order to bring out that if the lack *has* its place [*le manque a sa place*] in this atomistic topology of the signifier, that is, if it occupies therein a specific place of definite contours, the order would remain undisturbed. (PT, p. 45.)

While thus criticizing the hypostasis of a lack—the letter as the substance of an absence (which is not what Lacan is saying)—Derrida is illustrating what Lacan *is* saying about both the materiality and the localizability of the signifier as the mark of difference by operating on the letter as a material locus of differentiation: by removing the little signifier " ´ ," an accent mark which has no meaning in itself.[13]

The question of the nature of the "lack," however, brings us back to the complexities of the meaning and place of the "phallus." For while it is quite easy to show the signifier as a "difference" rather than a "lack," the question becomes much trickier in relation to the phallus. There would seem to be no ambiguity in Lacan's statement that "clinical observation shows us that this test through the desire of the Other is not decisive insofar as the subject thereby learns whether or not he himself has a real phallus, but insofar as he learns *that the mother does not*" (*Ecrits,* p. 693; translation and emphasis mine). The theory seems to imply that at some point in human sexuality, a referential moment is unbypassable: the observation that the mother does not have a penis is necessary. And therefore it would seem that the "lack" is localizable as the substance of an absence or a hole. To borrow a joke from Geoffrey Hartman's discussion of certain solutionless detective stories, if the purloined letter is the mother's phallus, "instead of a whodunit we get a whodonut, a story with a hole in it."[14]

But even on this referential level, is the object of observation really a lack? Is it not instead an interpretation—an interpretation ("castration") not of a lack but of a *difference?* If what is observed is irreducibly anatomical, what is anatomy here but the irreducibility of difference? Even on the most elementary level, the phallus is a sign of sexuality as difference, and not as the presence or absence of this or that organ.

But Lacan defines the phallus in a much more complicated way. For if the woman is defined as "giving in a love-relation that which she does not have," the definition of what the woman does not have is not limited to the penis. At another point in the discussion, Lacan refers to "the gift of what one does not have" as "love" (*Ecrits,* p. 691). Is "love" here a mere synonym for the phallus? Perhaps; but only if we modify the definition of the phallus. Love, in Lacan's terminology, is what is in question in the "request for love" ("demande d'amour"), which is "unconditional," the "demand for a presence or an absence" (*Ecrits,* p. 691). This "demande" is not only a reference to "what the Other doesn't have," however. It is also language. And language is what alienates human desire such that "it is from the place of the Other that the subject's message is emitted" (*Ecrits,* p. 690). The "demande" is thus a request for the unconditional presence or absence not of an organ but of the Other in answer to the question asked by the subject from the place of the Other. But this "demande" is not yet the definition of "desire." Desire is what is left of the "demande" when all possible satisfaction of "real" needs has been subtracted from it. "Desire is neither the appetite for satisfaction, nor the demand for love, but the difference which results from the subtraction of the first from the second, the very phenomenon of their split [*Spaltung*] " (*Ecrits,* p. 691). And if the phallus as a signifier, according to Lacan, "gives the *ratio* of desire," the definition of the phallus can no longer bear a simple relation either to the body or to language, because it is that which prevents both the body and language from being simple: "The phallus is the privileged signifier of that mark where logos is joined together with the advent of desire" (*Ecrits*, p. 692; all translations in this paragraph mine).

The important word in this definition is *joined*. For if language (alienation of needs through the place of the Other) and desire (the remainder that is left after the subtraction of the satisfaction of real needs from absolute demand) are neither totally separable from each other nor related in the same way to their own division, the phallus is the signifier of the articulation between two very problematic chains. But what is a signifier in this context? "A signifier," says Lacan, "is what represents a subject for another signifier." A signifier represents, then, and what it represents is a subject. But it only does so for another signifier. What does the expression "for another signifier" mean, if not that the distinction between subject and signifier posed in the first part of the definition is being subverted in the second? "Subject" and "signifier" are coimplicated in a definition that is unable either to separate them totally or to fuse them completely. There are three positions in the definition, two of which are occupied by the same word, but that word is differentiated from itself in the course of the definition—because it begins to take the place of the *other* word. The signifier for which the other signifier represents a subject thus acts like a subject because it is the place where the representation is "understood." The signifier, then, situates the place of something like a reader. And the reader becomes the place where representation would be understood if there were any such thing as a place beyond representation; the place where representation is inscribed as an infinite chain of substitutions whether or not there is any place from which it can be understood.

The letter as a signifier is thus not a thing or the absence of a thing, not a word or the absence of a word, not an organ or the absence of an organ, but a *knot* in a structure where words, things, and organs can neither be definably separated nor compatibly combined. This is why the exact representational position of the letter in the Minister's apartment both matters and does not matter. It matters to the extent that sexual anatomical difference creates an irreducible dissymmetry to be accounted for in every human subject. But it does not matter to the extent that the letter is not hidden in geometrical space, where the police are looking for it, or in anatomical space, where a literal understanding of psychoanalysis might look for it. It is located "in" a *symbolic* structure, a structure that can only be perceived in its effects, and whose effects are perceived as repetition. Dupin finds the letter "in" the symbolic order not because he knows where to look, but because he knows *what to repeat*. Dupin's "analysis" is the repetition of the scene that led to the necessity of analysis. It is not an interpretation or an insight, but an act—an act of untying the knot in the structure by the repetition of the act of tying it. The word *analyze,* in fact, etymologically means "untie," a meaning on which Poe plays in his prefatory remarks on the nature of analysis as "that moral activity which disentangles" (Poe, p. 102). The analyst does not intervene by giving meaning, but by effecting a *dénouement.*

But if the act of (psycho-)analysis has no identity apart from its status as a repetition of the structure it seeks to analyze (to untie), then Derrida's remarks against psychoanalysis as being always already *mise en abyme* in the text it studies and as being only capable of finding *itself,* are not objections to psychoanalysis but a profound insight into its very essence. Psychoanalysis is, in fact, itself the primal scene it seeks: it is the first occurrence of what has been repeating itself in the patient without ever having occurred. Psychoanalysis is not the interpretation of repetition; it is the repetition of a *trauma of interpretation*—called "castration" or "parental coitus" or "the Oedipus complex" or even "sexuality"—the traumatic deferred interpretation not *of* an event, but *as* an event that never took place as such. The "primal scene" is not a scene but an interpretative infelicity whose result was to situate the interpreter in an intolerable position. And psychoanalysis is the reconstruction of that interpretative infelicity not as its interpretation, but as its first and last act. Psychoanalysis has content only insofar as it repeats the dis-content of what never took place.

But, as Dupin reminds us, "there is such a thing as being too profound. Truth is not always in a well. In fact, as regards the more important knowledge, I do believe that she is invariably superficial" (Poe, p. 119). Have we not here been looking beyond Lacan's signifier instead of *at* it? When Lacan insists on the "materiality of the signifier" that does not "admit partition," what is *his* way of explaining it? Simply that the word *letter* is never used with a partitive article: you can have "some mail" but not "some letter".

> Language delivers its judgment to whoever knows how to hear it: through the usage of the article as partitive particle. It is there that the spirit—if spirit be living meaning—appears, no less oddly, as more available for quantification than the letter. To begin with meaning itself, which bears our saying: a speech rich with meaning ["plein *de* signification"], just as we recognize a measure of intention ["*de* l'intention"] in an act, or deplore that there is no more love ["plus *d'amour*"]; or store up hatred ["*de la* haine"] and expend devotion ["*du* dévouement"], and so much infatuation ["tant *d*'infatuation"] is easily

reconciled to the fact that there will always be ass ["*de la* cuisse"] for sale and brawling ["*du* rififi"] among men.

But as for the letter—be it taken as typographical character, epistle, or what makes a man of letters—we will say that what is said is to be understood *to the letter* [*à la lettre*], that *a letter* [*une lettre*] awaits you at the post office, or even that you are acquainted with *letters* [*que vous avez des lettres*] —never that there is *letter* [*de la lettre*] anywhere, whatever the context, even to designate overdue mail. (SPL, pp. 53-54.)

If this passage is particularly resistant to translation, that is because its message is in the "superficial" play of the signifier. Like the large letters on the map which are so obvious as to be invisible, Lacan's textual signifier has gone unnoticed in the search for the signified, "signifier."

But the question of translation in connection with a message so obvious that it goes unseen is not an accident here. For in his discussion of Dupin's statement that "'analysis' conveys 'algebra' about as much as, in Latin, *'ambitus'* implies 'ambition,' *'religio,'* religion, or *'homines honesti'* a set of *'honorable* men'" (Poe, p. 212), Lacan asks:

Might not this parade of erudition be destined to reveal to us the key words of our drama?[15] Is not the magician repeating his trick before our eyes, without deceiving us this time about divulging his secret, but pressing his wager to the point of really explaining it to us without us seeing a thing. *That* would be the summit of the illusionist's art: through one of his fictive creations to *truly delude us*. (SPL, pp. 50-51.)

But the trick does not end here. For has Lacan himself not slipped into the paragraph on the quantification of the letter a parade of "key words" for his reading of the situation? "Full of meaning," "intention," "hatred," "love," "infatuation," "devotion," "ass for sale," and "brawling among men"—all of these words occur as the possible "signifieds" of "The Purloined Letter" in the "Seminar." But if the key words of a reading of the story thus occur only in the mode of a play of the signifier, the *difference* between "signifier" and "signified" in Lacan's text, as well as in Poe's, has been effectively subverted. What the reader finally reads when he deciphers the signifying surface of the map of his misreading is: "You have been fooled." And in this discussion of "being fooled" Lacan, far from excluding the narrator, situates him in the dynamic functioning of the text, as a reader *en abyme* duped by Dupin's trick explanations of his technique; a reader who, however, unconscious of the nonsequiturs he is repeating, is so much in awe of his subject that his admiration blinds *us* to the tricky functioning of what he so faithfully transmits.

To be fooled by a text implies that the text is not constative but performative, and that the reader is in fact one of its effects. The text's "truth" puts the status of the reader in question, "performs" him as its "address." Thus "truth" is not what the fiction reveals as a nudity behind a veil. When Derrida calls Lacan's statement that "truth inhabits fiction" an unequivocal expression or revelation of the truth of truth (PT, p. 46), he is simply not seeing the performative perversity of the rest of the sentence in which that "statement" occurs: "It is up to the reader to give the letter . . . what he will find as its last word: its destination. That is, Poe's message deciphered and coming back from him, the reader, from the fact that, in reading it, he is able to say of himself that he is not more feigned than truth when it inhabits fiction" (*Ecrits*, p. 10; translation mine). The play between truth and fiction, reader and text, message and feint, has become impossible to unravel into an "unequivocal" meaning.

We have thus come back to the question of the letter's destination and of the meaning of the enigmatic "last words" of Lacan's "Seminar." "The sender," writes Lacan, "receives from the receiver his own message in reverse form. Thus it is that what the 'purloined letter,' nay, the 'letter in sufferance' means is that a letter always arrives at its destination" (SPL, p. 72). The reversibility of the direction of the letter's movement between sender and receiver has now come to stand for the fact, underlined by Derrida as if it were an *objection* to Lacan, that there is no position from which the letter's message can be read as an object: "no neutralization is possible, no general point of view" (PT, p. 106). This is the same "discovery" that psychoanalysis makes—that the analyst is involved (through transference) in the very "object" of his analysis.

Everyone who has held the letter—or even beheld it—including the narrator, has ended up having the letter addressed to him as its destination. The reader is comprehended by the letter; there is no place from which he can stand back and observe it. Not that the letter's meaning is subjective rather than objective, but that the letter is precisely that which subverts the polarity "subjective/objective," that which makes subjectivity into something whose position in a structure is situated by an object's passage through it. The letter's destination is thus *wherever it is read:* the place it assigns to its reader as his own partiality. Its destination is not a place, decided a priori by the sender, because the receiver is the sender, and the receiver is whoever receives the letter, including nobody. When Derrida says that a letter can miss its destination and be disseminated, he reads "destination" as a place that preexists the letter's movement. But if, as Lacan shows, the letter's destination is not its literal addressee, nor even whoever possesses it, but whoever is possessed by it, then the very disagreement over the meaning of "reaching the destination" is an *illustration* of the nonobjective nature of that "destination." The rhetoric of Derrida's differentiation of his own point of view from Lacan's enacts that law:

> Thanks to castration, the phallus always stays in its place in the transcendental topology we spoke of earlier. It is indivisible and indestructible there, like the letter which takes its place. And that is why the *interested* presupposition, never proved, of the letter's materiality as indivisibility was indispensable to this restricted economy, this circulation of property.
>
> The difference I am *interested* in here is that, a formula to be read however one wishes, the lack has no place of its own in dissemination. (PT, P. 63; translation modified, emphasis mine.)

The play of "interest" in this expression of difference is too interesting not to be deliberate. The opposition between the "phallus" and "dissemination" is not between two theoretical objects but between two interested positions. And if sender and receiver are merely the two poles of a reversible message, then Lacan's very substitution of *destin* for *dessein* in the Crebillon quotation—a misquotation that Derrida finds revealing enough to end his analysis upon—*is,* in fact, the quotation's message. The sender (dessein) and the receiver (destin) of the violence which passes between Atreus and Thyestes are equally subject to the violence the letter *is.*

The reflexivity between receiver and sender is, however, not an expression of symmetry in itself, but only an evocation of the interdependence of the two terms, of the *question* of symmetry as a *problem* in the transferential structure of all reading. As soon as accident or exteriority or time or repetition enters into that reflexivity—that is to say, from the beginning—"Otherness" becomes in a way the letter's sender. The message I am reading may be either my own (narcissistic) message backward or the way in which that message is always traversed by its own otherness to itself or by the narcissistic message of the other. In any case, the letter is in a way the materialization of my death. And once these various possibilities are granted, none of them can function in isolation. The question of the letter's origin and destination can no longer be asked as such. And whether this is because it involves two, three or four terms must remain undecidable.

The sentence "a letter always arrives at its destination" can thus either be simply pleonastic or variously paradoxical; it can mean "the only message I can read is the one I send," "wherever the letter is, is its destination," "when a letter is read, it reads the reader," "the repressed always returns," "I exist only as a reader of the other," "the letter has no destination," and "we all die." It is not any one of these readings, but all of them and others in their incompatibility, which repeat the letter in its way of reading the act of reading. Far from giving us the "Seminar"'s final truth, these last words enact the impossibility of any ultimate analytical metalanguage.

If it at first seemed possible to say that Derrida was opposing the unsystematizable to the systematized, "chance" to psychoanalytical "determinism," or the "undecidable" to the "destination," the positions of these oppositions seem now to be reversed; Lacan's apparently unequivocal ending says only its own dissemination, while "dissemination" has erected itself into a kind of "last word." But these oppositions are themselves misreadings of the dynamic functioning of what is at stake here. For if the letter is what dictates the rhetorical indetermination of any theoretical discourse about it, then the oscillation between unequivocal statements of undecidability and ambiguous assertions of decidability is one of the letter's inevitable effects. For example, the "indestructibility of desire," which could be considered a psychoanalytical belief in the return of the *same,* turns out to name repetition as the repetition not of sameness but of *otherness,* resulting in the dissemination of the subject. And "symbolic determination" is not opposed to "chance": it is what emerges as the *syntax* of chance.[16] But "chance," out of which springs that which repeats, cannot in any way be "known," since "knowing" is one of its effects. We can therefore never be sure whether or not "chance" itself exists at all. "Undecidability" can no more be used as a last word than "destination." "Car," said Mallarmé, "il y a et il n'y a pas de hasard." The "undeterminable" is not opposed to the determinable; "dissemination" is not opposed to repetition. If we could be sure of the difference between the determinable and the undeterminable, the undeterminable would be comprehended within the determinable. What is undecidable is whether a thing is decidable or not.

As a final fold in the letter's performance of its reader, it should perhaps be noted that, in this discussion of the letter as what prevents me from knowing whether Lacan and Derrida are really saying the same thing or only enacting their own differences from themselves, my own theoretical "frame of reference" is precisely, to a very large extent, the writings of Lacan and Derrida. The frame is thus framed again by part of its content; the sender again receives his own message backward from the receiver. And the true otherness of the purloined letter of literature has perhaps still in no way been accounted for.

Notes

Opening Remarks

1. Jacques Derrida, "La différance," *Théorie d'Ensemble* (Paris: Seuil, 1968), pp. 51-52. Translation is my own.

2. For a cogent, sustained analysis of theory's *meaningful* way of missing its target and of the significant richness of the effects thereby produced, see (apropos of Austin's theory of speech acts) Shoshana Felman, *Le scandale du corps parlant: Don Juan avec Austin, ou la séduction en deux langues* (Paris: Seuil, 1980).

Chapter 1

1. Roland Barthes, *S/Z*, trans. Richard Miller (New York: Hill and Wang, 1974), pp. 15-16.

Chapter 2

1. Stéphane Mallarmé, *Oeuvres complètes* (Paris: Pléiade, 1945), pp. 285-86. All translations from Mallarmé are my own.

2. Cf. Roger Dragonetti, "*Le Nénuphar blanc*: A Poetic Dream with two Unknowns," *Yale French Studies*, no. 54 (1977) (special issue on Mallarmé).

3. See Jacques Derrida, "La double séance," *La dissémination* (Paris: Seuil, 1972). (My English translation of the foregoing will be published as *Dissemination* by The University of Chicago Press in 1981.)

4. See Jacques Lacan, *Ecrits: A Selection*, trans. Alan Sheridan (London: Tavistock, 1977), p. 284: "It is Freud's discovery that gives to the signifier/ signified opposition the full extent of its implications: namely, that the signifier has an active function in determining certain effects in which the signifiable appears as submitting to its mark, by becoming through that passion the signified."

147

Chapter 3

1. The complete texts of these two poems will be found appended to the end of this chapter.

2. Charles Baudelaire, *Les Fleurs du Mal,* critical edition by Jacques Crépet and Georges Blin (Paris: Corti, 1950), p. 387. All translations from the French are my own.

3. Suzanne Bernard, *Le Poème en prose de Baudelaire à nos jours* (Paris: Nizet, 1959), p. 144.

4. Alison Fairlie, "Observations sur les *Petits poèmes en prose,*" *Revue des Sciences humaines,* 127 (July–Sept. 1967): 453.

5. Charles Baudelaire, *Oeuvres complètes* (Paris: Pléiade, 1961), p. 736. (Hereafter referred to as *O.C.*)

6. The violence involved in this struggle is often literalized in Baudelaire's prose poems. In *La Soupe et les nuages,* for example, the transition between the "lyricism" of the clouds and the "realism" of the soup is a "violent punch in the back."

7. Pierre Fontanier, *Les Figures du discours* (Paris: Flammarion, 1968), p. 99.

8. Cf. Roman Jakobson, *Fundamentals of Language* (Paris: Mouton, 1971), p. 90: "The development of a discourse may take place along two different semantic lines: one topic may lead to another either through their similarity or through their contiguity. The *metaphoric* way would be the most appropriate term for the first case and the *metonymic* way for the second. . . . In normal verbal behaviour both processes are continually operative."

9. *O.C.,* p. 737.

10. Cf. Emile Benveniste, *Problèmes de linguistique générale* (Paris: Gallimard, 1966), pp. 251, 256: "La notion de 'personne' . . . est propre seulement à *je/tu,* et fait défaut dans *il.* . . . La 'troisième personne' est bien une 'non-personne.'"

11. Madame de Staël, *De l'Allemagne,* quoted by Antoine Adam in his edition of *Les Fleurs du Mal* (Paris: Garnier, 1961), p. 271.

12. Emanuel Swedenborg, *Les Merveilles du ciel et de l'enfer* (Berlin: J. Decker, 1782), 1:64.

13. Cf. Michel Deguy, "La poésie en question," *Modern Language Notes,* 85, no. 4 (May 1970): 421.

14. *O.C.,* p. 687.

15. *O.C.,* pp. 617–18.

16. Emmanuel Kant, *The Critique of Judgement* (Oxford: Clarendon Press, 1952), p. 185.

17. Paul Valéry, *Oeuvres complètes* (Paris: Pléiade, 1957), 1:1510.

18. *O.C.,* p. 685.

19. Roman Jakobson, "Linguistics and Poetics," in *Style in Language,* ed. Thomas A. Sebeok (Cambridge: MIT Press, 1960), p. 356.

20. Karl Marx, *Capital* (New York: International Publishers, 1967), p. 67; emphasis mine.

21. Georges Blin, "Les Fleurs de l'impossible," *Revue des Sciences Humaines,* 127 (July–Sept. 1967): 461.

22. Bernard, *Le Poème,* p. 140.

23. J. B. Ratermanis, *Etude sur le style de Baudelaire* (Basel: Editions Art et Science, 1949), p. 442.

24. Bernard, *Le Poème,* p. 144.

25. Henri Brugmans, *"L'Invitation au voyage de Baudelaire,"* *Neophilologus* 30 (Jan. 1946): 12.

26. Fairlie, "Observations," 453.

27. Letter to Jules Troubat, February 19, 1866 (*Correspondance* [Paris: Pléiade, 1973], 2:615).

28. It is not without interest here to mention that at this period in French history the conservative political party of the upper bourgeoisie was called "the Party of Order" and preached, above all, "public tranquillity."

29. Cf. *La Dédicace* ("Tout est à la fois tête et queue . . . nous pouvons *couper* où nous voulons"); *La chambre double* ("Mais un *coup* terrible, lourd a retenti à la porte, et . . . il m'a semblé que je recevais un *coup* de pioche dans l'estomac"); *La soupe et les nuages* ("Et tout à *coup* je reçus un violent *coup* de poing dans le dos"); *Mlle Bistouri* ("à moins que ce ne soit pour te *couper* la tête . . ."); *Le Galant tireur* ("la poupée fut nettement *décapitée*"); *Assommons les pauvres* ("D'un seul *coup* de poing, je lui bouchai un oeil. . . . Je *cassai* un de mes ongles à lui *briser* deux dents"), etc. In addition, the majority of the prose poems are themselves "cut" by a *but* or *however* which marks the passage from one code to another, or from an affirmation to its reversal.

30. Georges Blin, *Le Sadisme de Baudelaire* (Paris: Corti, 1948), p. 171.

31. "Une coupure pure sans négativité, un *sans* sans négativité et sans signification," Jacques Derrida, "Le sans de la coupure pure," *Digraphe* 3 (1974): 13.

32. Marx, *Capital*, p. 71.

33. This expression appears in Baudelaire's sonnet *La Beauté*, where Beauty, depicted as a statue, proclaims: "Je hais le mouvement qui déplace les lignes."

34. Cf. *Le fou et la Vénus*, in which an artist-clown begs for mercy from a statue of Venus and which ends: "Mais l'implacable Vénus regarde au loin je ne sais quoi avec ses yeux de marbre."

Chapter 4

1. Robert G. Cohn, *Toward the Poems of Mallarmé* (Berkeley and Los Angeles: University of California Press, 1965), p. 147.

2. Remy de Gourmont, *Promenades littéraires* 4th ser. (1912): 8. All translations from the French are my own.

3. Cf. Stéphane Mallarmé, *Oeuvres complètes* (Paris: Pléiade, 1945), pp. 366, 645, 859.

4. Ibid., pp. 38, 366, and 382.

5. J. L. Austin, *How to Do Things with Words* (Cambridge: Harvard University Press, 1975), p. 6.

6. Ibid., p. 14.

7. Ibid., p. 8.

8. Ibid., p. 92.

9. Ibid., p. 63.

10. Ibid., p. 60.

11. Emile Benveniste, *Problèmes de linguistique générale* (Paris: Gallimard, 1966). p. 274.

12. Paul Larreya, "Enoncés performatifs, cause, et référence," *Degrés* 1, no. 4 (Oct. 1973): m23.

13. Richard Klein, "Straight Lines and Arabesques: Metaphors of Metaphor," *Yale French Studies* 45 *(Language as Action)* (1970).

14. As Ursula Franklin points out *(Anatomy of Poesis: The Prose Poems of Stéphane Mallarmé* [Chapel Hill: University of North Carolina Press, 1976]), the period after "d'abord" in the Pléiade edition is a typographical error: it is the speech itself which is being modified by the expression "invariable et obscur."

15. *Oeuvres complètes*, p. 366: "The pure (poetic) work implies the elocutionary disappearance of the poet, who leaves the initiative to words. . . ."

16. Austin, *How to Do Things with Words*, p. 76.

17. Austin, "Performative Utterances," *Philosophical Papers* (London: Oxford University Press, 1970): 241.

18. Austin, *How to Do Things with Words*, p. 22.

19. Ibid., p. 28. An attempt to study the return from a conventional to a "natural" authority among human beings would produce something like the film *Swept Away*, which is set on Austin's desert island: this return would inevitably be reversed by language—in this case by the suspension of an act by the word *no*, uttered not by the victim but by the perpetrator of the act.

20. Cf. Mallarmé's description of the word *société* in "Sauvegarde," *Oeuvres complètes*, p. 419: "La Société, terme le plus creux, héritage des philosophes, a ceci, du moins, de propice et d'aisé que rien n'existant, à peu près, dans les faits, pareil à l'injonction qu'éveille son concept auguste, en discourir, égale ne traiter aucun sujet ou se taire par délassement."

21. See, in addition to the excellent list given by Ursula Franklin: Charles Mauron, *Mallarmé l'obscur* (Paris: Corti, 1968), and Austin Gill, *Mallarmé's Poem "La Chevelure vol d'une flamme . . ."* (Glasgow: University of Glasgow, 1971).

22. Cf. *Oeuvres complètes*, p. 367: "Tout devient suspens, disposition fragmentaire avec alternance et vis-à-vis, concourant au rythme total lequel serait le poème tu."

23. This is, of course, a radical rereading of the notion of rhyme in Mallarmé as set forth, for example, in the following in *Oeuvres complètes*, p. 365: "L'acte poétique consiste à voir soudain qu'une idée se fractionne en un nombre de motifs égaux par valeur et à les grouper; ils riment: pour sceau extérieur, leur commune mesure qu'apparente le coup final". Whereas previous readers have emphasized the idea of resemblance implied by the expression "motifs égaux," I would emphasize the idea of fragmentation implied by the expression "se fractionne," in order to show that it is the combined incompatibility of these two emphases that constitutes Mallarmé's notion of rhyme.

Chapter 5

1. Stéphane Mallarmé, *Oeuvres complètes* (Paris: Pléiade, 1945), p. 385. All translations from Mallarmé are my own.

2. ΜΑΘΗΜΑΤΙΚΗ ΣΥΝΤΑΞΙΣ·

3. Jacques Lacan, *Ecrits*, trans. Alan Sheridan (London: Tavistock, 1977), p. 165 (translation slightly modified).

4. Noam Chomsky, *Aspects of the Theory of Syntax* (Cambridge: MIT Press, 1965), p. 53.

5. Letter to Maurice Guillemot, quoted by Jacques Scherer, *L'Expression littéraire dans l'oeuvre de Mallarmé* (Paris: Droz, 1947), p. 79.

6. See also Julia Kristeva, *La Révolution du langage poétique* (Paris: Seuil, 1974).

7. One example among hundreds: In his "Cantique de Saint Jean," Mallarmé uses the instant of decapitation in order to discuss the relation between head and body in terms of the opposition between up and down. The syntax of the poem is such that we are never able to determine whether the head is rising or falling. This indeterminacy is produced by numerous ambiguities. Depending, for example, on whether the word *que* in the phrase "qu'elle s'opiniâtre à suivre" introduces a subjunctive command or a relative clause, the poem is saying either "que la tête s'opiniâtre à suivre son pur regard là-haut" or "la tête refoule ou tranche les anciens désaccords avec le corps qu'elle s'opiniâtre à suivre." It is equally plausible, therefore, to see the head rising up after its *pur regard,* or falling down in reconciliation with the body. For a more detailed analysis of the effects of such ambiguities, see Chapter 4, above.

8. Jean Piaget, quoted in Ruth Tremaine, *Syntax and Piagetian Operational Thought* (Washington, D.C.: Georgetown University Press, 1975), p. 7.

9. Guillaume Apollinaire, *Alcools* (Paris: Gallimard, 1920), p. 78. Translation is my own.

Chapter 6

1. E. L. Grant Watson, "Melville's Testament of Acceptance," *New England Quarterly* 6 (June 1933): 319-27; the expression appears in both John Freeman, *Herman Melville* (New York: Macmillan Co., 1926), p. 136 and in Raymond M. Weaver, *The Shorter Novels of Herman Melville* (New York: Liveright, 1928), p. li; William E. Sedgwick, *Herman Melville: The Tragedy of Mind* (Cambridge: Harvard University Press, 1944), pp. 231-49; F. Barron Freeman, *Melville's "Billy Budd"* (Cambridge: Harvard University Press, 1948), pp. 115-24.

2. Joseph Schiffman, "Melville's Final Stage: Irony," *American Literature* 22, no. 2 (May 1950): 128-36; Philip Withim, "*Billy Budd*: Testament of Resistance," *Modern Language Quarterly* 20 (June 1959): 115-27; Karl E. Zink, "Herman Melville and the Forms—Irony and Social Criticism in *Billy Budd*," *Accent* 12, no. 3 (Summer 1952): 131-39; Lawrance Thompson, *Melville's Quarrel with God* (Princeton: Princeton University Press, 1952).

3. Kenneth Ledbetter, "The Ambiguity of *Billy Budd*," *Texas Studies in Literature and Language* 4, no. 1 (Spring 1962): 130-34; S. E. Hyman, quoted in R. H. Fogle, "*Billy Budd*—Acceptance or Irony," *Tulane Studies in English* 8 (1958): 107; Edward M. Cifelli, "*Billy Budd*: Boggy Ground to Build On," *Studies in Short Fiction* 13, no. 4 (Fall 1976): 463-69.

4. Lee T. Lemon, "*Billy Budd*: the Plot Against the Story," in *Studies in Short Fiction* 2, no. 1 (Fall 1964): 32-43.

5. John Middleton Murry, "Herman Melville's Silence," *Times Literary Supplement,* 10 July 1924, p. 433.

6. Herman Melville, *Billy Budd*, in *Billy Budd, Sailor, and Other Stories*, ed. Harold Beaver. (New York: Penguin Books, 1967), p. 405; emphasis mine. Unless otherwise indicated, all references to *Billy Budd* are to this edition, which reprints the Hayford and Sealts reading text.

7. It is interesting that reversibility seems to constitute not only *Billy Budd*'s ending but also its origin: the *Somers* mutiny case, which commentators have seen

as a major source for the story, had been brought back to Melville's attention at the time he was writing *Billy Budd* by two opposing articles that reopened and retold the *Somers* case, forty-six years after the fact, in antithetical terms.

8. Charles Weir, Jr., "Malice Reconciled," *Critics on Melville*, ed. Thomas Rountree. (Coral Gables, Fla.: University of Miami Press, 1972), p. 121.

9. Freeman, *Melville's "Billy Budd,"* p. 73.

10. William York Tindall, quoted in William T. Stafford, ed., *"Billy Budd" and the Critics* (Belmont, Calif.: Wadsworth, 1969), p. 188.

11. Lewis Mumford, quoted in Stafford, *"Billy Budd" and the Critics*, p. 135.

12. Schiffman, "Melville's Final Stage," p. 133.

13. Richard Chase, *Herman Melville: A Critical Study*, excerpted in Stafford, *"Billy Budd" and the Critics*, p. 174.

14. Ibid., p. 173.

15. Otto Fenichel, *The Psychoanalytic Theory of Neuroses*, quoted in ibid, p. 176.

16. Edwin Haviland Miller, *Melville* (New York: Persea Books, 1975), p. 358.

17. Ibid., p. 362.

18. Rollo May, *Power and Innocence* (New York: W. W. Norton, 1972), pp. 49-50.

19. John Middleton Murry, quoted in Stafford, *"Billy Budd" and the Critics*, p. 132.

20. Tindall, *"Billy Budd" and the Critics*, p. 187.

21. John Seelye, *Melville: the Ironic Diagram* (Evanston, Ill.: Northwestern University Press, 1970), p. 162.

22. Kingsley Widmer, *The Ways of Nihilism*: A Study of Herman Melville's Short Novels (Los Angeles: Ritchie, Ward, Press, for California State Colleges, 1970), p. 21; Hannah Arendt, *On Revolution* (New York: Viking Press, 1963), pp. 77-83; Widmer, *Nihilism*, p. 33; Milton Stern, *The Fine Hammered Steel of Herman Melville* (Urbana: University of Illinois Press, 1957), pp. 206-50; Weir, "Malice Reconciled," p. 121; Withim, *"Billy Budd,"* p. 126; Weir, "Malice Reconciled," p. 121; Thompson, *Melville's Quarrel*, p. 386; Weir, "Malice Reconciled," p. 124; Leonard Casper, "The Case against Captain Vere," *Perspective* 5, no. 3 (Summer 1952): p. 151; Weir, "Malice Reconciled," p. 121; Thompson, *Melville's Quarrel*, p. 386; James E. Miller, *"Billy Budd*: The Catastrophe of Innocence," *MLN* 73 (March, 1958): p. 174; Widmer, *Nihilism*, p. 29.

23. See especially pp. 34-35, Editors' Introduction, *Billy Budd, Sailor* (Chicago: University of Chicago Press, 1962).

24. Thomas Paine, *The Rights of Man* (Garden City: Anchor Press, 1973), p. 303.

Chapter 7

1. Edgar Allan Poe, *Great Tales and Poems of Edgar Allan Poe*, (New York: Pocket Library, 1951); hereafter designated as "Poe". Jacques Lacan, *Ecrits* (Paris: Seuil, 1966); quotations in English are taken, unless otherwise indicated, from the partial translation in *Yale French Studies* 48, *(French Freud)*, 1973; hereafter designated as "SPL". Jacques Derrida, published in French in *Poétique* 21 (1975) and, somewhat reduced in *Yale French Studies* 52 *(Graphesis)*, 1975; unless otherwise indicated, references are to the English version, hereafter designated as "PT."

2. Such a concatenation could jokingly be called, after the nursery rhyme, "This is the text that Jacques built." But in fact, it is precisely this kind of sequence or chain that is in question here.

3. We will speak about this bracketed signature later; for the time being, it stands as a sign that Derrida's signature has indeed been added to our round robin.

4. "So infamous a scheme/If not worthy of Atreus, is worthy of Thyestes."

5. *La politique de l'autruiche* combines the policy of the ostrich (*autruche*), others (*autrui*) and Austria (*Autriche*).

6. Jacques Derrida, *Positions* (Paris: Minuit, 1972), pp. 112-13; translation is my own; Ibid., p. 113.

7. Jacques Lacan, *Ecrits* (Paris: Seuil ["Points"], 1966), pp. 11; translation is my own.

8. Cf. Lacan's description in *Ecrits*, p. 60, of the "effect of disorientation, or even of great anxiety," provoked by these exercises.

9. Some idea of the possibilities for misunderstanding inherent in this question can be gathered from the following: In order to show that psychoanalysis *represses* "writing" in a logocentric way, Derrida quotes Lacan's statement against tape recorders: "But precisely because it comes to him through an alienated form, even a retransmission of his own recorded discourse, be it from the mouth of his own doctor, cannot have the same effects as psychoanalytical interlocution." This Derrida regards as a *condemnation* of the "simulacrum," a "disqualification of recording or of repetition in the name of the living and present word." But what does Lacan actually *say*? Simply that a tape recording *does not have the same effects* as psychoanalytical interlocution. Does the fact that psychoanalysis is a technique based on verbal interlocution automatically reduce it to a logocentric error? Is it not equally possible to regard what Lacan calls "full speech" as being *full* of precisely what Derrida calls *"writing"*?

10. Paul de Man, *Blindness and Insight*, (London: Oxford University Press, 1971), p. 140.

11. Stanley E. Fish, "How Ordinary is Ordinary Language?," *New Literary History*, 5, no. 1: 52.

12. In a final twist to this *mise en abyme* of writing, the words "by L. L. de Loménie" have been penciled into the Yale library's copy of this book under the title in a meticulous nineteenth-century hand, as the book's *"supplément d'origine"*.

13. It is perhaps not by chance that the question here arises of whether or not to put the accent on the letter *a*. The letter *a* is perhaps the purloined letter *par excellence* in the writings of all three authors: Lacan's "objet *a*," Derrida's "différance," and Edgar Poe's middle initial, *A*, taken from his foster father, John Allan.

14. Geoffrey Hartman, "Literature High and Low: the Case of the Mystery Story," *The Fate of Reading*, (Chicago: University of Chicago Press, 1975): 206.

15. *Ambitus* means "detour"; *religio*, "sacred bond"; *homines honesti*, "decent men." Lacan expands upon these words as the "key words" of the story by saying: "All of this . . . does not imply that because the letter's secrecy is indefensible, the betrayal of that secret would in any sense be honorable. The *honesti homines*, decent people, will not get off so easily. There is more than one *religio*, and it is not slated for tomorrow that sacred ties shall cease to rend us in two. As for *ambitus:* a detour, we see, is not always inspired by ambition" (SPL, p. 58).

16. This is what the mathematical model in the "Introduction" of the "Seminar" clearly shows; beginning with a totally arbitrary binary series, a syntax of regularity emerges from the simple application of a law of combination to the series. When

it is objected that that syntax *is not,* unless the subject *remembers* the series, Lacan responds in *Ecrits,* p. 43: "That is just what is in question here: it is less out of anything real . . . than precisely out of *what never was,* that what repeats itself springs"; translation mine. Memory could thus be considered not as a *condition* of repetition, but as one of its syntactic effects. What we call a random series is, in fact, already an *interpretation,* not a given; it is not a materialization of chance itself, but only of something which obeys our conception of the laws of probability.

Index of Names and Works